The Day the World Fell Out of My Bottom

by Norman Will

All proceeds from the sale of this book will go to
Cancer Research UK

Typeset in Adobe Caslon Pro and Cronos Pro

Design and publishing by UK Book Publishing

www.ukbookpublishing.com

ISBN: 978-0-9926433-7-9

Acknowledgements

To my sisters, Joyce and Noreen. Without Joyce I wouldn't
be here and the book would never have materialised.

To the whole clan of the Ewan family of Hillyland,
Perth. I see you as an extension of my own kin.

To Dr Marie Weir (Philosophy) who posed me many
helpful questions in relation to writing my book.

To all the medical staff who have come to my rescue
and helped me in various clinics – sorry, but you
are all too numerous to mention individually.

My pal Elaine Gamble who had faith
and trust in me from early on.

To Trevor Woods who has been a stalwart
friend – please don't ever change.

To my wife, for her love and support for the first 15 years
together. The last 3 years with you were hellish, however.

To my Aunt, Wilma McFarlane, for trying
to cheer me up by singing to me.

To all the patients I have met and who gave
me courage and inspiration. Thank you.

To my editor Linda Innes, thank you for the
great job. I always felt I was in safe hands.

And lastly, to my dogs, past and present, in chronological
order: Sheba, Sasha 1, Samson, Sasha 2, Jess, Scooter,
Sabre, Max (all long-haired German Shepherd
Dogs) and my Westie Terrier, Duncan – the only
one still with me. You can never underestimate the
healing and therapeutic qualities of dogs. Mine have
kept me going over the years and given me so many
happy memories. I miss my dogs who are no longer
with me. I hope to be reunited in the next life.

The more people I meet, the more I like my dogs.

My thanks to Christina Davey for helping me find a way
to publish this book and arranging the cover artwork.

To the girl from Blair Athol - I never realised the
true value of what I held until it was way too late.

Introduction

Bang!
Bang!
Bang!

The blows came in hard and sure, and each one found its mark. I was immediately left reeling, dazed, confused and nauseated.

This was September 1989 and I was sitting in Northampton General Hospital in a Doctor's office. I had just been told that I had Non-Hodgkin Lymphoma, a type of cancer, and that it was in its final stage: stage four, that there was not a lot they could do for me and that I might only live for another five years.

I was twenty five years old.

The Doctor's delivery of the news was brutal and without compassion. I was summarily dismissed and told to expect a letter in the post. To the Doctor I was just another statistic on a medical chart. Twenty-three years later I'm still a statistic on a medical chart and a great big anomaly.

I don't know how I got home that day. All I know is that this is my story – and my name is Norman Will.

Chapter 1

It's the 1st July, 2012. Sophie has agreed to talk about the medical side of my illness. I'm grateful to her for that, because I know she finds it all very difficult, so just to say, 'thanks'. I've got a number of questions I'm going to ask about it all, and hopefully, she can do her best. She's got a good memory.

Norman: So. Sorry this has been dragged up, but there we are. So my first question was: in the years prior to the transplant, what were the effects, the symptoms?

Sophie: Well, it used to come and go intermittently. And for most of the time, you were extremely well, because you could go to the gym, go to martial arts, go out on your bike. You could go to work and do all the things that you wanted to do; but intermittently, your main symptom was the swelling in all of your lymph glands in your body. But the ones you were aware of were those in your neck, the ones in front of your ears, on the side of your cheeks, and the ones in your arms and in your groin.

Obviously, you didn't really have any symptoms from the swelling of the lymph glands inside your body, like in your chest or in your abdominal cavity, but you were aware of the ones on the outside. And I

1

don't think they were especially painful. They were a bit sore, maybe, a bit tender, but you used to get quite distressed that the ones on your face and on your neck were noticeable. And I think that was your main symptom, from what I can remember. Oh, and sometimes you used to get tired.

Norman: What treatment was I on, for this?

Sophie: You used to be mainly on Chlorambucil: chemotherapy taken in tablet form, and in those days they used steroids in a very, very high dose, so you'd also be on 80 mgs of Prednisolone, which is an awful lot when you think about it. Nowadays, you'd maybe consider 20 mgs to be a very high dose. So the Chlorambucil and the Prednisolone were the mainstays of your treatment. I think some time shortly after we'd met, you were on an injection called Interferon. Don't know if you remember that?

Norman: No.

Sophie: Don't remember it at all?

Norman: I remember it now that you've mentioned it, but yeah, it's vague.

Sophie: Yeah. And you had to give it to yourself. I don't think it was every day, it might have been twice a week or something like that. You had to inject it into your leg, and it gave you flu-like symptoms, so you had quite aching joints and felt quite tired on the Interferon. That was quite a long course, but I seem to remember that your lymphoma progressed while you were on that, so you ended up back on the Chlorambucil and Prednisolone, and they stopped the Interferon injections. So those were your main physical symptoms, I suppose.

Norman: Right, okay. And how was I coping mentally with this? The anger that's followed me throughout my illness, was it present at that point? Was I, you know... was I controlling it? How was that going?

Sophie: I think ever since I've met you, you've been a very angry person about your illness, and maybe about other things to do with your upbringing, as well. It may be just your personality – that's just the way you react to things, but I can remember you always being very angry, quite enraged at some points, in fact, and quite emotionally labile, I suppose. Just as you are now.

Norman: What does that mean? I don't understand that.

Sophie: Which bit don't you understand?

Norman: Labile.

Sophie: Labile: up and down.

Norman: Right.

Sophie: Like, up and down with your moods. So, one day
            you might be angry and shouting, and very cross
            about the whole thing. And then, just as quickly, you
            might be feeling very low and tearful… very upset
            about things. So expressing the same emotions in a
            different way, I suppose, alternating between the two.
            But yes, I think you've always been very angry about
            it.

In 1980s, my friend Jim and I went down to the Kent
Custom Motor Cycle show in Dimchurch, taking
the opportunity to visit Jim's sister and her boyfriend,
Bally, who had a job working on the Channel Tunnel.
Afterwards, I left Jim spending time with his sister and
headed north back home to Perth. I came up by the M25
and M1 on my bike, on my ownsome, and I'd done over
200 miles by the time I got to Northampton and decided
it was time to have a break.

I chose Northampton for two reasons. One: because
it was there, and two: I had a very tenuous connection
with a girl I'd gone out with in Perth who had moved to
Northampton to seek her fame and fortune; so I thought,
it's as good a place as any to stop. I came off at Junction
15, up the slip road and up to Queen Eleanor's Cross. I got
a lovely view of Northampton from there, and it looked
as though Northampton was laid out in a bowl from
that angle. I thought the city was a massive metropolis. I
suppose when you're a small town lad at heart you're pretty

impressed by the size of large towns and cities!

I remember the weather was glorious. It was one of those days when you're happy to be alive! I had no worries – well, no job, either, but no real worries and I was full of hope. I put the Kawasaki into gear and trundled off into the town centre for a coffee, a bite to eat and to see what it was like before heading off home to Perth again. I got into the town and found a little space to park.

No sooner had I parked and got my helmet and back-pack off, when I felt this tap on my shoulder, and – would you believe it? It was this girl I used to know in Perth – Anne! She told me that since she'd moved to Northampton, she had had plenty of work and money. There were loads of jobs in the town and surrounding areas for electricians, if I was interested, she said. I told her I'd been paid off – made redundant – so at her suggestion, I decided to check out the job situation in Northampton. We spent lunchtime together and exchanged phone numbers.

When Anne left, I went off and I bought the local rag, *The Chronicle and Echo*, and sat in the sunshine taking down the particulars of the adverts I was interested in. I spotted a job for an electrician with a company called HR Mann, based in St Andrews Road. I bought an A-Z, fired the bike up and drove down to there. I went into the office, explained that I was passing through and didn't really have time to arrange an interview, but if they were willing to interview me there and then, I was available. The boss duly met with me and chatted to me for a while. He offered me a job with his company and said if I wanted the job, I could start on the following Monday! The pay was good enough, too, so I thought 'Christ, I'd better get some digs!' So, I went back to the local rag, looking at the page with rooms to let and found a little B&B up in the Abingdon area of Northampton which I thought seemed nice.

The B& B was in a little terraced house and the owners were just letting one of their bedrooms. I went to see the couple, Denise and Frank, and asked them to excuse the way I was dressed – in my biker's gear and probably looking a bit grubby. The woman was pleasant, and told me she came from Dudley. Her husband was Irish. I stayed with them that night and set off back to Perth the next day. I felt really pleased! I'd only just arrived in Northampton and I'd already got a job and some digs! I had a really good first impression of Northampton and I thought the women were really pretty. The buildings were nice, too. So, yeah, I liked Northampton.

I was very excited when I drove home to Perth to pack my bags and pick up my tools ready to head back down south for my new job the following Monday. I got home on the Friday night, knackered, put the bike in my mum's garage and went for a few beers, then home to bed at eleven o'clock. I was in bed, when, around 3am there was a loud knock on the door at mum's house where I was staying.

It was the police, telling me that someone had broken into mum's garage.

"We have recovered your motorbike. Did you know it had been stolen?"

"Well, no, I didn't know it had been stolen!" I scowled. As if I'd be lying blissfully in bed, instead of hunting down the thief like a dog!

Although my bike had been recovered, it had been pretty smashed up in a crash, while the person who nicked it managed to get away with just a few scratches. The only reason he was caught was because the police just happened to be coming in the opposite direction on a routine patrol and saw the whole thing.

When the coppers arrived, I'd asked them who'd nicked my bike and they told me it was this guy, Beany McLaren, from across the street – a neighbour. He must have seen me coming home and putting the bike away in the garage.

I had taken this quite well, "Ah, well!" I roared. "When I get hold of that little bastard, I'll kill him!"

"Sir, I'm afraid we can't have you making threats like that," the young copper reprimanded me seriously, as if he was reading from his police bible.

While the older copper said, "When you get hold of him, give him a good kicking for us, too. He's always in trouble and forever in the nick. I know where you're coming from, mate," He leaned in confidentially, tapping the side of his nose with the flat of his index finger, "but keep it to yersel'."

So – 'good cop, bad cop'!

Many years later, I met Beany McLaren at a football match – St Johnstone V. Dundee United. It was a cup semi-final, played in Dunfermline's ground. Beany was standing behind me so I turned round, thumped him and burst his nose. I got dragged away by the polis.

The policeman asked, "What did you start fighting like that for? He didn't do anything to you! "

"He nicked my bike and smashed it up… and caused me a whole lot of trouble!" I said, fuming. "He's a thieving, junkie bastard!"

The polis shrugged, "Och, well, you probably did the right thing, then!"

And he let me go! It was the only time I've ever thumped someone.

So there I was, with a job in Northampton to go to, digs sorted out, and no way of getting there for the Monday. Absolute bloody nightmare! Fortunately, Michael, a good friend of mine owned an old Ford Escort as well as having a company car. He came to the rescue and gave me his old silver Escort. Unremarkable car, but you know what? It didn't matter. It was a godsend. I will be eternally grateful to Michael for that. I had the benefit of a borrowed car for the foreseeable future, so I packed my tools and my bag of clothes into the boot and headed back to Denise and Frank's terraced house in Northampton, ready to start my new job with H R Mann on time!

I'd been away from home before. The first time was when I was 21, when I went to Aldershot, through the Job Centre. If I agreed to go to Aldershot, the Job Centre said they'd get me a job as an electrician and give me a few hundred pounds to help get me started. It was a government initiative. Remember Secretary of State for Employment, Norman Tebbit, telling people to "get on your bike" for a job? Well, I was the other Norman!

I must have got down to Northampton late on Sunday afternoon when I unpacked my suitcase. Since I had the car, it meant that I could take my entire wardrobe with me : all of two jackets, two pairs of jeans and two pairs of shoes. I probably had more tee shirts, socks and pants. To be fair, I wasn't the sharpest dresser in town! I went out for a wander round the local area after unpacking. It was a lovely sunny evening and I discovered that a lovely park: Abingdon Park, was close to my digs. More importantly, I also discovered the Abingdon pub, which became one of my haunts for the next two or three months.

In the B&B I had a cosy wee room. Frank, the Irish owner, was a big tall guy; a salesman who basically felt that everyone was giving him grief. He used to come home and drink, and tell me about all the trouble he'd had that day. Denise was from Dudley in the West Midlands, "Not Birmingham!" she insisted, and they had an old Collie dog. They were decent enough folks with a nice clean house and I had a neat, clean room. I only had fifty pounds in my pocket, which I gave to Denise for my digs. I had no money left for fags, beer or food, but I was glad I had my bed and breakfast covered, at least until the Thursday of my first week. So that's what I did with my last fifty quid – gave it to my landlady! She was kind enough to make me spam sandwiches, which I thought were going to be bloody awful, but I tell you – you'll eat anything if you're hungry. They tasted great, by the way. There I was in Northampton with a couple of bags of clothes, two boxes of tools, a borrowed car and no money.

But I was excited!

On my first day at work, I told the boss my predicament – I couldn't work a 'lie week' because my dig money would be due and I'd no money coming in. The boss was good about it and said 'not to worry' as he would pay me my wages at the end of the week. So that was kind of him, and good for me.

For the first job, I was sent to a school on the north side of Northampton that was being rewired. This is where I first met Trev. He arrived in Northampton the week before me and because neither of us knew anyone, we became friends, although I think Trev had an Uncle Allan who lived in Northampton but he was just leaving for America. Trev got me into a whole lot of bother. The school was for Sixth Form girls who were about eighteen years old and we were twenty-three. Trevor shouted to the girls to: "Get their tits out for the lads!" and of course the girls reported the incident, saying a guy with a northern accent had shouted these comments at them. I had only been there a week when I was removed from site because I was blamed. Of course I didn't 'shop' Trevor. I did tell the boss that it wasn't me who called out to the girls, but I wouldn't say who it was. Anyway, somebody had to take the fall. I fell. It didn't turn out too bad. I was sent to Barclay's and was given the job of replacing old fluorescent light fittings, which was a bit of a doss job. You certainly didn't need to be an electrician to do it. There were lots of girls working at Barclay's that you could flirt with, without fear of them running off to tell a tutor.

So that was the start of my friendship with Trevor

and we frequently went out together for curries and beer. Neither of us knew anyone else, really. It became a ritual that we went out on a Friday night, got 'pished' and on our way home, we'd get a curry. We were always trying to outdo each other to see who could eat the hottest curry. It got to a ridiculous point where basically we were just asking for curried chilli – a 'phal'– and it was just madness! I don't know if we even tasted what we had to eat, let alone enjoyed it – it was just mingin' hot! We both came to an unspoken agreement that we would go back to normal curries, because it was just getting out of order, really!

I had also taken all my karate gear with me to Northampton and started looking for a club straight away. I found a couple, but they were Wadoryu. I used to do Shotokan Karate and various other things, but training is training. So off I popped and took myself along to a new club and really enjoyed myself. I used to do a bit of karate teaching myself in Northampton.

In my first digs Denise and Frank, as I mentioned, owned an old Collie dog like Lassie. One night, when Frank wasn't at home, the dog took a turn for the worse, so I sat downstairs with him, as Denise was too upset. The dog passed away in the kitchen, which was really sad. I cleaned up the dog mess and told Denise that he had died peacefully. He just took one last big breath, let it all go and passed on to 'dog heaven,' I hope. All dogs deserve to go to heaven, probably.

By now, I had been at Frank and Denise's for about three months when I decided that it was time to change my accommodation and share with other young people. I was living in someone else's home and felt that it was time for me to become more independent.

Another guy from Scotland, Rennie, arrived on the scene, unemployed and looking for work. He was married, though separated, with two kids. He had great plans to get himself sorted out and to make things work between him and his wife but ultimately that never happened. It just wasn't going to work out.

I got a house up in Barrack Road in Northampton, a three storey Edwardian affair. Rennie moved into the same address, too, and had the room next to mine on the top floor. The landlord wanted a month's rent as deposit, as well as four weeks' rent up front. Rennie and I could either pay the rent or the deposit, but we didn't have enough to pay both. So, the Landlord did us a favour and waived the deposit, which was good of him. My room was ok; it had a bed, a chest of drawers, a wardrobe, cheap carpet, but it was freshly painted throughout.

Me and Rennie had a room each in this house and the other three rooms were let to three Occupational Therapy students. The landlord lived on the ground floor. He was an Egyptian chap, an amiable person who played the double bass. It was at this address that the borrowed Escort got its window panned in by vandals. I went to bed one night, woke up the next morning to find the back window smashed. What money I'd saved since arriving in Northampton had to be used to pay for replacing the window. That was a bit of a shame, really.

Trev and I played the odd game of squash. He used to come over to our flat and play cards or board games, or listen to music with me and Rennie. We never had much money between us. We all came from nothing and by the time we'd paid our rent and bought food, we rarely had much money left, so we didn't go out much – maybe once or twice a week for a few beers. I was enjoying myself, though. It was quite a good time in my life as I was excited about being away from home, living on my own, doing my own thing. I also tried to save a little money, where I could.

I got about £600 from the insurance company for my Kawasaki. It had been written off, so I salvaged it from the insurance company, buying it back off them as scrap, for £150. I was saving up to get it repaired. The bike needed a new engine, crank cases, handlebars, and clocks. The tank needed repairing too. The bike was pretty well buggered, really, but I didn't want to let it go. I took the bike to my pal Bob Moss, who had a motorcycle workshop in the old Territorial Army buildings in Perth. He said he'd fix it up. He took months and months and months to fix it, and I was on the point of saying to him that I'd take it somewhere else, when he eventually let me know it was fixed.

My main thought had been to stay in Northampton and work until I had enough money to pay for my bike to get fixed. I thought I'd be home to Perth within six months, but I kind of got used to the money and never made it back home to live in Perth. And as I said, the girls seemed to be very pretty in Northampton. Anne and I had started to see each other again, in an on/off sort of relationship, which suited us both at the time. There was nothing too serious about it. We'd ring each other up if either of us wanted to go to the cinema or for a drink.

Trevor and I were getting on alright, and we decided to go self-employed working through the agencies. Companies were paying up to a couple of pounds more per hour for agency staff and we'd heard wonderful stories about working this way. We never worked as permanent employees for a company again, for many years after that. We enjoyed the experience of working for agencies, but it was a bit precarious. We never knew where we were going to end up!

One of our jobs was working in a borstal, on the coast in Suffolk. We were booked in to stay at this old seventeenth century coaching inn. It was all wooden beams, sloping floors, uneven ceilings and walls. It was a lovely old building.

A chap from BT who was also staying at the inn said he had a lot of cannabis with him. He invited himself back to Trev's and my room to smoke this stuff. Although I was twenty three, I had never touched drugs in all my life, but I thought, 'Oh well, in for a penny in for a pound! I'll try anything once' – except bestiality and incest! So we were all smoking this pot. Trevor and the BT guy passed out, but I was awake the whole time. I just felt fuckin' awful!

After a bit of time, I drifted asleep myself, intermittently dozing and waking up. One of the times I awoke, there was all this crashing and banging going on outside. I looked out through the window and saw trees and dustbins flying past the window. We weren't even on the ground floor! These things were flying past at roof height! I thought, 'Christ! I'm hallucinating. I'm never smoking that stuff again!' I felt ill, so I just closed my eyes, praying to wake up normal, and fell back to sleep!

In the morning I got up, not feeling too bright: cannabis and beer is not a good mix. I looked out of my bedroom window to witness utter devastation. Roofs taken off buildings, cars covered in tree branches, sheds smashed to pieces and debris everywhere. It was as if three drunk and drug-crazed lads had gone on a rampage and wrecked the streets around. I could barely recall what had happened.

It had been the night a hurricane hit Britain! The hurricane had well and truly hit, and Trevor and the BT guy had missed it all. Trevor never made it to his bed, still lying snoring on the carpet, and the BT guy never even made it back to his room. They'd been unconscious the whole time so they missed one of the greatest hurricanes in recent history! At least I saw it. Didn't believe it, but at least I saw it!

Trevor and I tried to get to work that morning, but there were trees down everywhere, lying across the road. It was just chaos, and so I think we gave up in the end as we couldn't get to borstal that day, for the blocked roads.

Anyway, back in Northampton, Trevor and I used to go to the Abingdon pub just around the corner from my digs. The pub was a lovely late Victorian building with a nice façade. It was smart inside, very clean and quite posh without being too obvious. There were various nooks and crannies to this pub, so you could have a quiet pint if you wanted or go into another room to listen to music, if you preferred. It was close to Abingdon Park which was nice, too. I played football in the park and also down at the race course, but that came later on.

I suppose that should have been a warning shot across the bows, as it were, because I remember when I was playing football, I often didn't feel right.

So, yeah, Trev and I hit it off and we used to go out boozing together to the Abingdon and a few other pubs and often grabbed a curry at the end of the night. Trevor's digs were one side of the park and mine at the other, so it was good for us both.

We used to go into town occasionally to drink in the Barrel Bar, which was a bit of a 'spit and sawdust' pub, but it suited us down to the ground. Then we used to go down to the Saddlers, and onto The King Billy – a bikers' pub which was a bit rough and ready, but we enjoyed it because if they didn't have a live band on, they used to play heavy rock music. The Saddlers was a bit of a shit-hole too, if I remember rightly. Trevor used to drink too much and land himself in bother, usually because he was chatting up some bloke's girlfriend and wouldn't leave her alone. The bloke would get annoyed and I would have to drag Trevor away and try and sort everything out. Trevor was a bit of a lad when it came to drink. He just couldn't hold it.

It would be too cruel and inaccurate to say he was legless, but he was nearly legless! Trevor's got an artificial leg. A wall fell on him when he was five years old, and he lost his leg as a result. He never complained or took advantage of his disability, always trying to work. He didn't claim disability allowance and before I was ill, I used to admire Trevor for his fortitude and for just getting on with it. People would never know he had a false leg because although he walked with a limp, he never made anything of it. In a way, he was my role model – absolutely.

There was another occasion when Trevor, Rennie and I were in the Barrel Bar in Northampton having a few beers. It was about 11 o'clock at night, so it was about shutting up time. We noticed a couple of guys picking on this one bloke and giving him a bit of a slapping. The fight got out of hand and the bloke was getting kicked from one end of the bar to the other. We stepped in to try and stop this but the two guys who were dishing out the beating had a couple of mates that we didn't know about, and they also stepped into the fight. There were about four of them against the three of us and the lad who had been getting beaten up never came to help us! Anyway, we tried to get these four guys outside but got caught behind two glass doors as the barman locked up.

After a few seconds, we thought, 'Where's Trevor?' Seemingly, he'd got caught outside the big glass doors and all we could see was Trevor getting his fuckin' arse kicked. Unfortunately, his artificial leg had fallen off inside the pub. So he was outside the pub – legless – and we were watching him through the glass doors. The barman wouldn't open the door to let him back in, as he didn't want the yobs getting back into the bar, so we were unable to do anything to help poor Trevor. The police were called and a newspaper reporter turned up. Trevor was pretty bruised up, but fortunately had no broken bones. The police took details and the newspaper reporter from the Chronicle and Echo interviewed Trev. Trev was quite made up with all the attention, until the next day when he read the headline of the newspaper article describing the fight with Trevor, which said: 'ONE LEGGED MAN WAS HOPPING MAD!' Trev and I still laugh about it!

Chapter 2

Norman: And how was my lymphoma presenting itself just
           prior to the transplant? What changed?

Sophie: Do you remember?

Norman: No.

Sophie: No. Well, what changed... what you noticed first in
           terms of physical symptoms, was that you got these
           lumps in your scalp. Do you remember those?

Norman: Mm. And they were painful.

Sophie: Yeah, they were painful. And do you remember they
           were red and scaly?

Norman: Mm.

Sophie: And they started quite small, but they grew really
           quickly. You went to see your GP about it and
           he thought it might be some form of psoriasis or
           eczema; he gave you some steroid lotion to put on
           them. Do you remember?

Norman: No.

Sophie: No. But they grew very quickly and were very painful
            and I suppose, knowing what I know now, that it was
            obviously a form of cutaneous or skin lymphoma,
            which for some bizarre reason was only manifesting
            itself on the scalp of your head, in your hair.

Norman: They were huge.

Sophie: They were like the size… what would you say? Like
            the size of half a plum, really, weren't they?

Norman: Half a golf ball.

Sophie: Half a golf ball or half a plum. And they grew very
            quickly, and eventually somebody – I suppose it
            must have been haematology – sent you for a biopsy
            of the one behind your right ear. Do you remember
            it? Dermatology?

Norman: I remember going…

Sophie: Yeah, it was in Northampton General, and they
            biopsied it under local anaesthetic; you've still got
            the scar there, behind your ear, from both the lump
            and the biopsy. And I think it was a very concerning
            time for you and for us, because we both kind of got
            an idea it was something to do with the lymphoma,
            because why wouldn't it be? And because of

            various things that people had said. But nobody

would come out and say, 'This is lymphoma
and it's changing the way it's presenting and it's
transforming.' And it was difficult, because you
were...

Norman: What were you thinking when we came out? Why
            didn't anybody say that the lymphoma has done
            this?

Sophie: Well, not wanting to be the one to break the bad
            news, I suppose...

Norman: Okay.

Sophie: ...would be the reason. But we tried, I remember. I
            tried, I asked people directly. In fact, I can remember
            asking one of them directly, 'Is this Norman's
            lymphoma?' because obviously you were very
            concerned about it. And they evaded the answer,
            saying, 'Oh well, you know, you'll have to wait for a
            biopsy to confirm.'

            They didn't really commit either way, and nobody
            was being very honest. And that was really difficult,
            because in that situation... even if your worst fears
            are realised, at least you know what's going on, and
            you can deal with it. There's nothing worse than
            trying to deal with major uncertainty. And it took
            quite a long time to get sorted out, as I recall, several
            weeks actually.

Norman: Do you think the fact of professionals being honest and upfront has really improved at all over the years, in the various departments I've been in?

Sophie: Yeah, I think it has, really. I think doctors have got better at answering honestly when questions are put to them. If you were in that situation now, you could say, 'So is this lymphoma?'

And they would look at it, and think 'Well, yeah, it probably is', and they'd say, 'Well, there's a very, very high chance that it is your lymphoma, which has changed, but I can't tell you that with 100% certainty until we've got a biopsy. So we're sending you to dermatology for a biopsy to confirm if it is the lymphoma. And if it is the worst case scenario and it's the lymphoma, then – just very briefly – X, Y, Z treatments are available.'

And clearly, that's better than a situation of nobody making eye contact with you, and nobody being very honest about it. It's still not perfect, but it's better than it was, since you ask the question.

Eye contact's important in more ways than one. One night, the three of us: me, Trevor and Rennie were in a pub in Gold Street in Northampton. We had had a few drinks but I remember the woman behind the bar was very slim, very blond, very attractive and very aware of it. Trevor kind of instantly fell in love with her. Me and

Rennie advised him that she was out of our league, telling him, "Don't even go there! You'll just make a complete twat of yourself!"

But, undeterred, Trevor had a few more beers, and then asked this girl out. To be fair to the girl, she was very polite and told Trevor that she already had a boyfriend so couldn't accept his offer. She gave Trevor the impression that if she hadn't had a boyfriend, she would've gone out with him. I don't think so! Trevor often carried on in that sort of vein. He was always approaching women who, it would be cruel to say were way out of his league. But they *were* way out of his league!

I liked Northampton. It was big, but not too big and I definitely thought the women were better looking here than the women in Perth. I don't mean that horribly, but they just were. They looked much happier. There was a big shopping centre in the middle of town and you could sit out at the main entrance and watch the world go by, or more specifically, watch the girls go by – and it was particularly good in the summer, when they wore fewer clothes!

The house in Barrack Road, as I've mentioned, was a three storey early Edwardian house.

It was nice and clean and within walking distance of the town and handy enough for most places. We got on well with the landlord, who lived on the ground floor, and used to help him out with jobs in the garden or around the house. With me being a 'sparky' and Rennie a glazier, we were both useful with our hands, so we sorted the landlord out, and he looked after us. It had been a nice enough building at one time, I suppose, but over time all the nice features had been ripped out. There were no fine fireplaces, for example, in any of the rooms.

I stayed in Barrack Road for quite some time and while I was there, I continued with my karate training and fell in with the crowd who trained at the club. There was a policewoman I got to know there called Susie, who had just bought a house with her pal. They were looking for someone to rent out their third room. It was a much bigger room than the one I had, so I told her that I was interested. Although the house was slightly further out of town, in a place called Sandes Barn, it suited me fine as I had the car and knew my way around Northampton by this time. I moved in with Susie and her friend Pippa. The housing estate was alright, a bit frayed round the edges but it had a boozer only two minutes from my front door. The Karate club was quite near the house too, so I used to come back to the house, drop my kit, and go for a pint after karate training. I lived at this address for three or four months and I still knocked about with Trevor, although by this time, he had a girlfriend who worked in the video store. At one point, Rennie and I had crashed at Trevor's digs for a while and when his landlady found out there were a couple of extras there, she was fuming. More later.

I remember Pippa asking if I would go as her partner to a party she'd been invited to in Sheffield. We stayed overnight and nothing untoward happened. I got on alright with Susie. Her choice of boyfriend was a bit unfortunate because I think it wrecked her career.

Although a policewoman herself, Susie was in trouble with the cops because she was seeing this criminal, which isn't acceptable in the police force. Basically, I think her bosses started leaning on her to get her to ditch him because he was just bad news. I met him a couple of times and didn't like him much. But then, I'm not a great fan of criminals!

Pippa, as I say, had taken me as her partner in Sheffield, and sometime later I asked if she wanted to come to the local for a drink, just as friends. As the old cliché goes, we had a drink, then one thing led to another and it all kind of got embarrassing in the morning and awkward thereafter. Ultimately, I thought it was better if I moved out. Pippa seemed a bit bitter about the whole thing so I thought it best to move on and put the whole episode behind me. I did notice, though, that Pippa had this friend, Rosetta, who was absolutely drop-dead gorgeous and I quite fancied her. However, I was smart enough to know that there was no point in getting to know her because she was Pippa's friend and after what had happened there, there was certainly no chance Pippa would ever put in a good word for me. So I steered clear after I'd transplanted myself. But I was hooked on Rosetta for a week or so!

Norman: Can you talk through the actual transplant itself, if you could?

Sophie: It was an older guy at Northampton. He didn't have brilliant communication skills, but you'd gone back to get the results of your biopsy, and they'd explained

to you that your lymphoma had transformed
from low grade, to being a high grade lymphoma.
And whilst this clearly wasn't a good thing, it did
mean that instead of just holding it at bay with the
Chlorambucil and the steroid tablets, now there
would be an opportunity to think about going for
a more radical treatment, which could potentially
be curative, and that would be a bone marrow
transplant. But they didn't do that in Northampton,
so they'd have to refer you up…

Norman: To Leicester.

Sophie: …to Leicester for that. And my impression was that
            happened pretty quickly, and that's when you met
            Dr Hutchinson…

Norman: That's right.

Sophie: …who was near retirement. A, nice old guy, who was
            the one and only transplant physician in Leicester.
            He worked on his own, didn't he, and he worked
            every day. Do you remember? He used to come in on
            Saturdays and Sundays as well. I seem to remember
            the first time we met him would have been on the
            unit. Do you think that's right?

Norman: No, we saw him in the clinic.

Sophie: I remember you being told that you'd need various tests and things, to make sure that you were fit to have it done, because it was a very gruelling treatment, and there was a chance that if you weren't fit enough, you wouldn't survive it. Do you remember that?

Norman: Yeah.

Sophie: Yeah. And so you had to have lung function tests and an echocardiogram.

Norman: Yeah, I remember that, because I was probably...

Sophie: And blood tests.

Norman: ...I was physically fit, even though I was ill.

Sophie: And I remember they told you it would involve chemotherapy and total body irradiation, and of course, finding a donor as well. So at that point, they must have asked you what family you had, who might be willing to donate, and they must have arranged the testing.

My sister Joyce would do anything for me. She and I spent a lot of time together and she took me everywhere with her when I was a kid. When Joyce went to College I seemingly went off the rails and was seen by a school psychologist because my behaviour was 'bonkers'. I put it down to the fact that Joyce was the person I related to best. Joyce took me out and bought me ice-cream and was nice to me and stuff and when Joyce went away to College, I felt there was nobody there for me. I had an older sister but she had a boyfriend and was married soon after. Joyce would just take me to the hockey or the running track. Sometimes we went swimming or to the cinema. My favourite film as a kid was the Sound of Music. I just went with her and she was happy to take me, so the bond was there. Joyce and I are very close.

Norman: So they find a donor in my sister, and then what happens, you know? How…? Obviously, they harvest my sister's bone marrow. What did they do to me? What's the prep before it goes in?

Sophie: Well, it all had to be very tightly coordinated, and I can remember thinking at the time, I don't know if this helps, but I remember that after they'd identified that Joyce was going to be a suitable donor for you, it seemed that it was all systems go after that, there seemed a real rush to get you in, do you remember?

Norman: Mm.

Sophie: It was very, very rushed. It was a whirlwind of investigations and tests and this, that and the next thing, getting things ready. There did seem to be some sort of pressure to get you in and have this transplant done. And looking back on it, I wonder actually, just how ill you were. Obviously, you didn't

28

feel desperately unwell, but as to how rapidly your lymphoma was advancing… and if you hadn't had the transplant, what the likely outcome would have been… Would you have just died? Because there did really seem to be some urgency to get on with it at all costs, because you had all those tests and they got Joyce sorted out quickly, and then they had to coordinate the chemotherapy and the irradiation, and collecting the stem cells from Joyce and stuff...

Norman: The transplant was carried out as near as possible to when they thought you would live until - so that if the transplant was unsuccessful, the medical profession had kept you alive as long as possible. I seem to remember, if I didn't have the transplant I would be dead within six months.

Sophie: Well, probably somebody told you that, and I would suspect that there wasn't really any other treatment that was going to work. It was this or nothing.

Norman: Yeah. That's what I was going to say. It was do or die.

Sophie: Yeah. And they did tell you that there was a 25% chance of dying as a result of the transplant. It was Lynn, the sister – one of the nurses, not any of the doctors – who just laid it on the line and said, 'Look, if you don't have it you're going to die. There is a 25% chance you will die, but a 75% chance you'll be alive at the end of it, which you won't be in six months if we do nothing...'

Hutch was just a bit kind of waffly, and he wouldn't lay it on the line like that, but Lynn would. Anyway, so we were sitting in the day room with Joyce and... what are you doing?

Norman: I saw a window fly. Sorry.

Sophie: ...Dave, and Margaret came in, and she said, 'Oh, Norman, because you're going to have irradiation, you've got to give a semen sample for storage', and she gave you a pot, which...

Norman: I remember that. I was actually upset because she'd discussed that...

Sophie: In a day room.

Norman: Yeah. In front of other people, rather than with just me, or me and my wife: me and you. So yeah, I thought she went about it the wrong way, but that aside.

Sophie: Yeah. So you were very upset about it, and quite rightly, because that was totally, totally inappropriate, and of course, what she didn't realise is that you'd had some tests done in Northampton which showed that you'd only got one or two sperm per sample. And so we hadn't really thought about this, what with all the upheaval and the tests and everything. And you kind of said, 'Whoa, whoa, whoa! Right, I'm putting a stop on this and I'm not going ahead with this until I've had a fertility consultation!'

And that really put the spanner in the works, because obviously, they were racing for the finish line, to get you in for this transplant, and you were refusing to go ahead and have it done. And this has brought back a memory I'd forgotten about. I remember, you did a sample at home, and I had to take it in to the Obs and Gynae department. I was a student then, and I had to take it into the Kensington building where I subsequently worked for 10 years, and I went and met Jane Blower, the embryologist there at the time. She still works there now, she's very senior. I gave your sample to Jane, and she took down your medical background and all of the details, and I think they thought, 'Oh, because your wife's a medical student, that'll be fine, just send her off with the sample and she'll get it sorted out.'

And she told me that there were very, very few live sperm there that they could store, and there was this new treatment called ICSI, where they inject a sperm into the egg, that potentially they could use, if they survived the freezing and if they were good enough quality, but she wasn't really sure.

But she said, 'The only thing to do is to get as many

samples as you can, in between now and going in for the transplant, and we'll store them. And then, as and when the time comes to use them, we'll see if they're good enough.'

Now, at the time, you were on Prednisolone and Chlorambucil when you gave those samples and when they stored them, so you were on chemotherapy, which clearly was another concern: what the effect of the chemotherapy would be on any resulting embryos. I can't remember how many samples we managed to take up to the hospital, but it was a few, between then and the transplant. I think you were still giving them in up until the point of going in. And, of course, now, they won't use samples given during chemotherapy at all, because now they know, 20 years later, that it's not a very good idea. But they didn't know that back then. So that was another thing which added to the stresses and strains of the pre-transplant days. I think I've got a bit off the point there.

Norman: Talk about the transplant procedure.

I suggested to Trevor around the time of leaving Susie's flat that since we were both paying digs/rent money, it might be a good idea to buy a house together somewhere, to share the costs and have something to show for our cash. So we duly started to do a bit of research and soon realised that we couldn't afford a house in Northampton, so we opted for Wellingborough , a little market town about twelve miles away. We saw a house we liked and got a hundred per cent mortgage on it.

When we first moved into our house we only had a few bits and bobs of furniture which included a sofa from my old gran's house and a little two-ring Baby Belling cooker from my mum. We used an old tea chest as a coffee table and had deck chairs to sit on. Trevor's contribution was a large plasma telly and a video recorder that he got by saving up his embassy fag coupons. For 25,000 coupons you got a telly, video recorder and lung cancer, obviously! Joyce's friends at the time, Pete and Evelyn Whitehall told me that they had furniture that they were throwing out and asked if I'd like to have it. So, given that they were in Edinburgh and we lived in Wellingborough, we hired a van and Trev and I went to collect this stuff. We arrived at Pete's and loaded the van with some pretty basic 70's stuff – chrome legged tables with glass tops – not really my taste but I thought "never look a gift horse in the mouth."

Then Evelyn asked if I'd like to give her some money towards it. I didn't really want the stuff particularly, never mind give her money, but I was too polite at the time to say no. Her request was made worse for me as my sister had given them furniture and didn't ask anything for it. The only things we ever used from all this stuff were the chrome legged table with the glass top as it was better than the tea chest, a coffee table – a big pine thing that looked like it had been made in a woodwork class at school and a couple of shelves. We went home a bit disappointed!

The other story linked to Pete was when Trev, me,

and by this time, Sophie, were all living together in Wellingborough. It was about 1992 and Pete had got my telephone number from Joyce and phoned me up to say he was in Northampton doing his helicopter pilot's license and wondered if he could take Sophie and I out for a meal.

I thought 'Great, nice to be treated!' and especially nice for Sophie as she was a poor student. So we met Pete in a smart 3 star hotel and had a tasty meal and wine. When the bill came it was about £180 and I felt relieved that we'd been invited out and that I wasn't picking the tab up. What I hadn't bargained for was picking up half the tab!

Pete said, "What will we do about this bill, will we just go halves?"

I was too polite to say anything other than, "Let me see what I've got…"

Sophie and I scraped all our money together which was the princely sum of about £70: our groceries money for a fortnight! I gave Pete the money and Sophie and I left absolutely furious.

Then at about half past midnight, Pete phoned, pished and said, "I didn't embarrass you did I?"

And again, being polite, I just said "No, no, we're fine, though I didn't think it would be so expensive."

What I should have said was, "You're a tight arsed git! Now, fuck off!"

But way back then, here we were, Trevor and I: the odd couple. Joint owners of a house in Wellingborough with a 100% mortgage. Happy as pigs in shit!

Sadly for me, I was diagnosed with Non-Hodgkin Lymphoma very soon after.

Sophie: The transplant procedure...

Norman: What did they do to me?

Sophie: Don't remember any of this? So after all this flurry,
            which had taken place over two weeks or whatever,
            the day finally came when you had to go. And
            they told you, you had to be in for 11.00 and what
            you had to take with you, and what to expect. I
            remember you got quite dressed up, for some reason.
            You'd put on your Chinos, and your shirt.

Norman: Blazer.

Sophie: Your blazer with gold buttons on, and your hat. And
            then you sat and had a cigar, a little, what do you call
            it?

Norman: Cheroot.

Sophie: Cheroot cigar, in the dining room of our house.

Norman: We've got a picture of that.

Sophie: Yes, we have, actually. The transplant day, that was
            when you went in, in the morning, and then we
            took you in with your sports bags and your dressing
            gowns. Remember, we'd bought you a dressing gown
            from M&S, Joyce had bought you the same one but
            in a different colour. A blue one and a green one.

And then we went in, and there was kind of nothing to be done, really. You went into your room, which was Room 1, the first room there, and we unpacked your stuff, and I suppose you must have had some obs done, blood pressure and all the rest of it.

Norman: Hang on a minute.

Sophie: Oh! Missed!

Norman: I saw a window fly. Go on.

Sophie: What's a window fly?

Norman: One that crawls up the window.

Sophie: Yeah. You had to go in regularly, because you'd got your Hickman line in. You had that done beforehand, as well.

Norman: Talk about the Hickman line.

Sophie: Talk about it now?

Norman: Yeah.

Sophie: So, prior to your transplant, you'd had to have a Hickman line put in, which is like a plastic tube, which tunnels up the skin of your chest. They put yours on your right side, didn't they? And it tunnels up your skin about four to six inches.

Norman: Above your nipple.

Sophie: Above your nipple, and then it just goes into
            you, just under your collarbone, into one of
            the big arteries there. And you received all your
            chemotherapy through that, your bone marrow,
            your fluids, any other drugs that you might need.
            Plus, they can use it for taking blood out, so you
            didn't have to have needles all the time once it was
            put in.

Norman: So that was kept in?

Sophie: So that was kept in, and obviously, that had to be
            maintained and kept clean and looked after. You had
            to wear a bandage round your neck to hold it up, do
            you remember? You had to sling it onto a bandage.

Norman: You could see it was filthy.

Sophie: It was. The bandage was disgusting.

Norman: Like Rab C Nesbitt would wear.

Leaving Scotland, at the same time as coming down south
I'd also toyed with the idea of going to Australia. My visa
was pretty much sorted out and I had the money I needed
saved up to guarantee me entry into the country. But then

I was diagnosed with non-Hodgkins lymphoma, which was a bit of a shit, really. Because I had this money in the bank, I thought 'I'll go out and buy a motorcycle', so I bought myself a Moto Guzzi Le Mans Mk 5. It was a nice bike and I enjoyed using it. I sold it a few years later and I never lost very much money on it – it held its price well.

The new job was alright and I'd met my new mate, Trevor. As I said earlier, we had been working in a school together till I got kicked off the work's site. Fortunately, I wasn't sacked, as they couldn't afford to lose their workers. My boss gave me a cushy job in Barclays office, changing all the light bulbs. So it worked out well for me and I enjoyed flirting with all the girls there!

When we first met, Trevor was telling me he was a great sports player, despite his artificial leg, and he reckoned he could beat me at squash. I had never played squash before, but that was pretty much like saying he could beat me with one leg tied behind his back, so I had to accept the challenge. I'd been doing all my karate training, so I was fit, but Trevor was so convinced of his skill that he reckoned he could stay still and have me running about the court like an idiot till he won.

So I said, "Let's have a small wager on this, then, Trevor."

"Ok then, a week's wages," he smirked, spitting on his hand, ready to shake on it.

"You're that confident, Trevor?" I asked doubtfully.

He said, "I'll beat you, no problem!"

"But you've got a false leg, Trevor," I reminded him, just in case he'd got carried away and forgotten.

"It doesn't matter," he grinned. "I'll just stand on one spot and I'll have you run ragged."

He never actually won a game. I beat him five games to nil! He was shocked and stunned! I never actually took his wages but I let him buy me a couple of pints. But that was Trevor –invincible, in his head – he believed he was never going to be beaten.

When Trevor and I went to Perth and we met my sister, Joyce. I think Trevor was on a 'jolly' tagging along with me, up to see my mum and have a break in Perth. We arranged to meet Joyce and little Sally, her daughter, who would have been about three at the time, in the Lamplight pub for a pub lunch. Trevor decided for reasons best known to himself to take his leg off to show Sally. Her face was a picture! She was transfixed by this man who could take his leg off, like a broken doll. After 23 years, Sally still refers to Trevor as "the man who takes his leg off" – it certainly has had a long lasting, possibly even psychologically traumatic effect. I don't know if she was frightened, but she still remembers that day quite clearly. It's just as well she's always had a great sense of humour and a robust psyche – otherwise, who's to know what psychological damage that action might have caused her? We're only glad she never became a serial killer or one of those scary porcelain doll-collectors, as a result.

I remembered the time that I was playing football and for some reason I couldn't run fast, which was strange as I used to be a reasonably good sprinter. I was playing out on the wing, but I must have been the slowest wing in the league that day. I should have questioned at the time why this was happening, since something was obviously wrong with me then! It was before the lumps appeared. I just didn't twig.

I was very healthy at this time and greatly involved with karate. You can start karate at any age, but because your bones are still developing up until your late teens, I believe it's better to wait till you're at least a teenager, as I did. I went to a very traditional karate school where everything was very disciplined and hard. I don't think young bodies are up to that rigour, but I started when I was seventeen. Some folk think seventeen is late, but it's not late to follow the curriculum, for want of a better word, because you've got to be strong. I mean, I've been to clubs where kids of eight and ten went, and they're not really grasping it. I chose karate as a sport because it was cheap – a pair of white 'pyjamas' and a couple of pounds per session. I never had money to buy expensive golf clubs! And my pal at the time, Craig Petterson, who was later my Best Man, had started karate about six months before me and he liked it. I joined around the time I lost my dad, actually. I kinda needed a focus at the time, and I took to karate like a duck to water. I got my Black Belt when I was twenty-one and continued training when I went to England and joined a number of clubs.

I always went in for competitions and the club I went to in Perth was recognised as one of the best karate clubs not just in Scotland, but in Great Britain. Both my instructors were excellent at karate – one was in the British squad and the other one was in the Scottish squad, so they had high standards. We were always graded by Japanese examiners. The club brought external examiners in, so we were assessed completely independently. There was a philosophy attached to karate and the club, and always a 'no-nonsense' approach. You didn't talk back to your instructors. You were very deferential to the black belts. They were always acknowledged, and you never questioned why you were doing what you were doing. The value at the core of the training was discipline – discipline held everything together. It didn't matter if someone was very good at karate or very poor at it, as long as the person's attitude was "I'm giving you 100%".

The karate school was well disciplined, unlike the school I went to. I played hooky but I was never a rogue at school; I knew it was good to keep a low profile and never have letters sent home to my parents. But karate was the first thing I ever felt I'd ever achieved anything in. I didn't see much point in school or trigonometry and all that. When I trained to become an electrician, that was a huge learning curve for me – I didn't know that there was so much involved, but again, when I went to college I never felt that half the stuff was of any relevance to my trade.

Now, Michael, who lent me his car, must have been in his early fifties when I first met him. I was sitting on the North Inch in Perth after being at my karate class with all my gear and Michael wandered over asking if I was going to be playing football. I thought the question was a bit strange as it was the middle of June.

I said, "No, the football doesn't start till August."

So we got chatting. It was a hot day; in fact, it was boiling and Michael said, "Do you want to go for a pint?"

I said ok, but to be honest I was wary. I suspected he might be trying to pick me up, but I thought, 'Well, he's in his fifties, I'm in my twenties – if he starts anything, I'll just thump him, basically.'

So we went for a beer and it turned out that he wasn't on the pick-up – he was just a nice guy. He worked for a company that created jobs for school leavers and he tried to persuade businesses to take on trainees, so he was interested in, and worked with, young people. He was a very clever man and wrote a lot of history books, including a book on the Clan McDougall.

Chapter 3

Sophie: I think the next day was when your chemotherapy
            started.

Norman: Right.

Sophie: And that dripped in, I can't remember if it was over
            several days or one day - I honestly can't remember.
            You had your chemotherapy. You were in hospital
            for exactly two weeks, as I recall. And then the next
            day, you must have had your total body irradiation,
            which was down in the old Victoria building, in the
            bowels of the hospital.

Norman: What does that involve? Irradiation?

Sophie: So, oh, you had to go for preparation for that as well,
            as part of your work up for your transplant, because
            they put a tattoo on your chest, didn't they?

Norman: Yeah. A little dot.

Sophie: A little dot. So... you'd had to go for a radiotherapy
            planning and work up at some point. I'd forgotten
            about that. But the total body irradiation was pretty
            quick. I went with you, and you went down on a
            trolley to where the concrete bunker was, where

they used to give the radiotherapy. You went into the radiotherapy room, still on your bed, and they centred your tattoo up with the laser beams, to make sure you were in the right place. I remember they let me round to watch you in the room, because obviously they can see you on a little video camera to make sure that you're okay. And you just had to lie still, and they pressed the button, and that was it done – in seconds. All you had to do was lie still.

Norman: How long did that treatment last?

Sophie: Seconds.

Norman: Really?

Sophie: Yeah, seconds. They just blasted you with radiation. Well, I don't know if you were feeling very well at that point, because you came out, and obviously, you've got to wait for a porter. You were lying on the trolley with your eyes shut, and I can remember I was trying to make sure you were covered up with blankets and tuck you in.

But you weren't in a very good mood, because you said really loudly, "Will you stop fucking pawing at me?"

Oh God, I just about burst into tears! It was awful.

Didn't know where to put myself. Anyway, so they took you back up to the room, but pretty shortly after that, you started to become very unwell from the chemotherapy and the radiation. And your hair started to fall out. Remember we got the clippers? And we shaved it all off one day. Do you remember, in Room 1?

Norman: Yeah.

Sophie: And I think you felt pretty ill.

Norman: Was I eating? Was I chucking up?

Sophie: No, not eating very much. Yes, being sick. But the main thing was your bowels. I remember the nurses were obsessed with your bowels, and you had to always show them what you'd done, as it were, which you were not very happy about one little bit. And you had green diarrhoea.

Norman: I'm not easy with bowel movements. I'm not easy about my bowel movements amongst strangers, as you found out.

Sophie: So having to go on the commode and show your bowel motions to the nurses upset you very greatly, and you moaned about that a lot, as I remember. You were supposed to use a commode, but you wouldn't, you kept going in the toilet and getting told off. And you were not well at all for two or three days. Then Joyce arrived at an agreed time, about three days later, to give her stem cells on the machine. She'd come up to stay with us. I'd made up our room for her to stay in, and I was going to stay on the sofa bed down in the front room, which she was not happy about, but I thought, 'Oh God, she's going to feel absolutely dreadful. She's not going to want to sleep on that uncomfortable sofa bed!'

And it was funny, because Joyce thought she was going to be absolutely fine, and I honestly thought she was absolutely not going to be fine. I can remember saying, "Oh, I'll give you a run up to the hospital and then I'll come and get you and take you home."

And she said, "No, no! When it's done, I shall walk into town, and go into Marks and Spencers and get something for us, for dinner, and then I shall walk home!" Which I do have to say I thought was a bit ambitious at the time.

Norman: Did she not realise the size of the needle?

Sophie: I don't know. She can talk about that, but of course, I was in my second year of medical school at this time, so I was still attending all of my duties, doing clinical stuff and things, trying to attend to you and Joyce and all I needed to attend to, and I was basically multi-tasking on a grand scale. So, yeah, I was still out in lectures and up the hill and down the hill to the medical school, to the hospital. So I do remember popping in to see Joyce, while she was on the machine, to make sure she was okay. And you were there, which was nice, giving her an egg sandwich, but bloody hell! Did she look green! Do you remember?

Norman: No. I don't remember any of this.

Sophie: Oh God, she was completely green around the gills, and I don't think she was feeling well at all, poor thing. On this machine with the two needles, one taking the blood in, and one taking the blood out. She passed out a couple of times, actually. And of course, she had to have the G-CSF injections, the granulocyte-colony stimulating factor injections, for a couple of weeks prior.

Norman: Can you say that a bit clearer?

Sophie: Gran-u-lo-cyte-col-ony stim-u-lating fact-or. G-CSF injections, to help the white blood cells to grow and be harvested, and I think they might have made her feel pretty crappy as well, but she'd have to comment on that, really. Anyway, so the offer of a lift home was accepted in the end - and she didn't go to Marks and Spencers and get dinner and walk home. She had a reasonable sleep and felt a bit better the day after.

Norman: When was I given her bone marrow? At what point after she had donated it? Straight away?

Sophie: Well, pretty much straight away, or maybe the next day after they'd, you know, cleaned it and done what they had to do with it.

            Oh! There's two!

Norman: Another small one. Yeah. Little buggers.

Sophie: Yeah, so when you received the stem cells, it was just like having a blood transfusion, really. It was just literally in a bag like a blood transfusion bag, and it just dripped in, over a few hours. And then there was an anxious wait for a few days, waiting to see if your blood cells engrafted, if they 'took', as it were. I suppose you would have been having daily blood tests, just to check what your blood counts were doing, make sure that they were actually going up, because new bloods cells were being produced. And they were watching out for symptoms of acute graft-versus-host disease. You did get that on your skin, on your hands and on your legs. You got the rash, and I suppose the diarrhoea carried on, as well. And you also had to be very careful not to be exposed to infection during that time.

Norman: So after two weeks, I was deemed well enough to go out.

Sophie: Yes. Once your neutrophil count – that's your
infection-fighting white blood cells – got above one,
you were allowed out. You were let out for a walk
once, do you remember?

Norman: Exciting.

Norman: We went across to Nelson Mandela Park.

Sophie: We went across to Nelson Mandela Park in all the
traffic, because we couldn't think of where else to
go. And there is nowhere nice to walk, as a patient,
around Leicester Royal Infirmary. It's a bit of a let-
down. I suppose with the new building it's better,
because they've got the terraces where you can sit
out. But you were allowed out into the fresh air. And
it was a reasonably nice day, it wasn't raining, it was
a bit blustery, bright, and we walked out, sat in the
park for an hour and then came back.

Norman: How was I looking, physically, comparing before the
transplant to post-transplant, in that fortnight? Was
there a huge difference?

Sophie: No, not really. I mean, I think the only change was
that you'd lost your hair. I suppose you'd probably
lost a bit of weight, and you were feeling a bit weak
and wobbly, but you didn't look particularly different,
from what I can recall. Yeah. I mean, after two weeks
you got home, and normal activity started to resume,

so apart from having to really be careful with making sure you didn't get an infection, you know, you were pretty much allowed to potter on as you had done before. So we had to boil all your water, or get bottled water. Make sure all your food was cooked properly. The house had to be kept very clean.

Norman: There were no takeaways allowed.

Sophie: No takeaways, so I had to cook everything. I had to make sure all the kitchen was cleaned every day, and the fridge was kept clean and all the rest of it, because they did bash on about infection. Plus, you were on quite a lot of tablets when you came home, your anti-rejection medication, which was Cyclosporin. Remember those big smelly tablets? Yeah? And then you were on blood pressure tablets, because Cyclosporin gives you high blood pressure. You were still on steroids, I believe, although not quite as many. And then you had a whole lot of other tablets, which were anti-infection tablets, basically; you had Penicillin, because your spleen had been irradiated, Aciclovir to guard against viruses, and Fluconazole for funguses. So you were on a fair whack of medicines when you came home, but you were quite well. You did well over the summer, if you remember.

Norman: Yeah.

Sophie: So you had to go in to the hospital, I think, twice a week, and then once a week, and you had to have tests for CMV virus. Blood tests every week. You had to have your Cyclosporin levels done, to make sure that your levels were not toxic, but therapeutic. So it was quite intensive, even after you were allowed home, really, the immediate post-transplant care.

You did well over the summer. People were ringing, and remember, you always used to say, "Oh yes, everything's going swimmingly." You used to say that to everybody over the summer. You were taking the dogs out for a walk and, you know, life was generally going on, really. And then, I don't really remember the sequence of events, but you came downstairs one day and you said you felt unsteady, dizzy, and you didn't feel quite right in your balance. Do you remember this at all?

Norman: No.

Sophie: No. And you had to take your temperature every day, didn't you? And report if your temperature went over 37.5 or something. So we'd done your temperature and that was normal, and you couldn't quite put your finger on it, but you weren't feeling very well. So we rang up the unit and they said to come in and get checked. I remember it being very vague in terms of symptoms, but they were concerned that you might have got meningitis. So

you ended up having a lumbar puncture – a spinal
tap, where you have to curl up into a ball.

Norman: Does that go up to 11?

Sophie: 12 sometimes. Where you have to curl up into a
ball, and they put a very fine needle into your spinal
column, and take off some of the fluid that cushions
your spinal cord.

Norman: Is that a painful procedure?

Sophie: I don't think it's especially painful, but it can
sometimes take quite a long time to do, it's very, very
fiddly, and you have to stay really still. So they sent
that off, and because they thought you'd got viral
meningitis, they treated you with Ganciclovir, strong
anti-viral medication into the vein, and you had to
stay in for that. But I don't think you were particularly
ill. It was also at that point that other problems
arose… it all kind of happened at around the same
time. You started to get more severe graft versus host
disease, yeah. And you remember, they changed you
from Cyclosporin to another newer anti-rejection
drug called Tacrolimus?

Norman: Yeah.

Chapter 4

I was starting to sleep more and more. We were
working in London at the time and travelled to and
from the job by train rather than driving. I once fell
asleep on the train and woke up in Derby, having been
all through Nottingham when I should have go off at
Wellingborough. I came home to Perth one weekend and
wasn't feeling brilliant but went out for a couple of pints
with my mates and became violently ill, being sick after
only a couple of beers, which wasn't like me. I enjoyed a
drink as a young guy, but never drank to the point of being
sick. That was very strange for me, and I've since found out
that the illness makes you alcohol intolerant.

The following day, I woke up, and all these lumps
had appeared. Joyce visited me at our mum's that same
weekend. She was teasing me about me taking over her
old bedroom when she stopped suddenly, having noticed a
lump on my neck.

She said, "Something's not right, Norman. Promise
me you'll go to the Doctor when you get back to
Wellingborough," which I did, and that was it.

My GP referred me to hospital straight away– no
course of antibiotics. Some people say their GPs are
rubbish, but I've always had great GPs. I have been
fortunate all the way through, in that respect. I was sent
to Northampton General Hospital. My own GP didn't
tell me what he thought it was, so at this point I wasn't

too worried. I wasn't in any pain, just had this constant tiredness, and I could fall asleep at the drop of a hat. This was really unlike me. I'd no energy for my training or much else, although I continued to work. I was still trying to do things as usual and although I knew things weren't right, I didn't think for a minute that it was cancer. At Northampton, I was referred to the Haematologist, who checked me over and took several blood samples.

After that I went in to get the results and they said, "Right, you've got something called Non-Hodgkin Lymphoma, which is a type of cancer. We'll send you a letter in the post. Good day, Mr Will."

There was no support, no talking it through, nor the offer of a cup of tea, or even "Would you like to go and sit somewhere quiet?"

I'd switched off as soon as they said I had this thing called lymphoma. I knew if you had something with an "-oma" or a syndrome, it was bad, and I thought you were pretty much finished. My life was turned on its head with no explanations.

I went home and was pretty numb. I made an appointment to see Dr Reid for the next day and he explained to me what Non-Hodgkin Lymphoma was. I wanted to turn to someone who loved me, and tell them what was going on and how I felt, and have them tell me it was all going to be alright. My dad would have been the one I turned to – he was always so laid back and mild, but he wasn't there to tell, because he was already dead. Telling my mum wasn't easy. I told her that I had cancer but she wasn't very warm, and never had been. I don't ever remember ever getting a hug from my mother, or even feeling that she really cared, in a loving way, possibly because she was brought up sternly, with no affection ever shown, and had never been given a hug when she was growing up. I used to be really angry about it, but now I can see probably why she was like that – although I wish she hadn't been. As a teenager it was difficult for me to appreciate how hard she had found her life, because of the impact her attitude had on me. Her coldness left me cold. I left home as soon as I possibly could, and went to Aldershot when I was twenty-one. I came back and stayed with my mother, just briefly, then lived with a girlfriend and soon I was off again. I didn't like to stay long.

Trev and I were living in Wellingborough at the time I was diagnosed. He was very supportive, as you will see.

Trevor came home, took one look at my expression and said, "What's up with you?"

I said, "I've got this cancer..."

And he said, "Thank fuck! I thought you had AIDS. Just think of the stigma that would have been attached to that!"

"What?"

He said, "Two blokes living in the same house and you've got AIDS? What would they think of me?"

I said, "Thanks, Trevor, for your support."

"That's alright, mate," he said. "Er... but when I say 'mate,' I mean, like, you know... Not..."

But that's just Trev, trying to cut it down to size. Trevor was in Wellingborough with me throughout the time I was having my treatment and he actually was a great support to me, believe it or not.

I never felt ill prior to the diagnosis. It just kind of crept up on me. Looking back, I realise that I did get signs so I think maybe I should have noticed them and done something about the first signs or taken the hint, like when I was playing football and couldn't run very fast. Also, I should've twigged that there was something wrong when I was sleeping at the drop of a hat. But you just don't. Or at least I didn't.

When this illness struck me, I didn't see myself as having a future. I had been told initially that I had 5 years left to live. At the age of 25 – that was a fifth of my life again, but when you're young and you were looking ahead to a long life, it's nothing. No time. No time at all.

I wasn't to know that they'd got it wrong, as it happens, and here I am, thirty years later. But you believe the experts, don't you? Usually. Until they're proven wrong. But at that time, there was everyone telling me that I would die, pretty soon. And until then, my life would be taken over by medical treatments and procedures, and drugs and pain. But the bottom line was – I was dying. Aged twenty five. Things to do before you're thirty. Things to do before you die.

Before I got my head round it all, I just went out and got blind drunk because, I thought, why not? What further harm can I do? Am I going to kill myself by wrecking my liver with a dozen pints? I'm going to be dead in 5 years anyway! Who cares?

And all the time I never realised that my anger and resentment was building up. There was no release for it, so sometimes it would erupt at the least provocation. If some guy was to accidentally bump into me passing by, instead of saying, "No problem," I'd furiously tell them to "Fuck off!" Then we would be squaring up to each other while Trevor would be dragging me off in one direction and the other guy's pal would be dragging him off in another. I would have happily got into a fight – anything to take out my seething anger on somebody, physically. I think the illness created negative energy in me at that time. If I could have channelled that energy into something positive, that would have been helpful, but I suppose I was in denial, then.

Later, as time went by, although thoughts of cancer kept coming back into my mind, at this point in my life I seemed to have boundless mental energy. Every time my mind drifted to thinking about having cancer I just came straight back at it by changing my thoughts to something more upbeat. That's the only way to live when they tell you you're dying. In fact, it's the only way to live. I am, as they say, the living proof.

In relation to dignity and confidentiality, with the NHS, you leave both at the front door when you enter. What gets me about the word 'confidentiality' and this dignity business, is that they basically don't exist, no matter how much they might say them. They're empty words, signifying nothing. They've got you on the ward, and the doctor comes around, and he draws the curtains around your cubicle for privacy. I call them the 'curtains of silence' – because obviously nobody can hear what you're saying at all to the doctor when the curtains are drawn, them being completely soundproofed and all, apart from the quarter of a millimetre thin fabric, the two foot gap at the bottom, the three foot gap at the top and the six inch gap in the opening between them. Then the doctor proceeds to ask you in an overly loud voice, just on the off-chance that you're deaf or daft, about your bowel movements, your waterworks and if you've got any bed sores. Of course, nobody else in the ward can hear what they are saying at all, because they've pulled the magic curtains around, which clearly means that everyone outside the inner sanctum is miraculously struck deaf! I don't know who the doctors are trying to kid! Me? The other patients? Themselves? Or what? Now they've introduced into Leicester Royal these even more magical red pegs – which mean that you've got 'pegs of privacy' on the 'curtains of silence.' These pegs are meant to be like garlic to vampires – they're a signal to keep people out and keep everything private, but of course nobody gives a shit. They think because they are a nurse a member of staff that it isn't meant for them – they are immune to it, and they poke their heads round anyway, so the pegs are a waste of time.

Before Sophie and I were married we used to go down to the homeopathic clinic. You're willing to try anything when you're told you're going to snuff it! Go for it, I say – go for homeopathic medicine if you think that it's going to help you. Do everything it takes. At that time we were staying in Wellingborough and I saw Dr Reid, my GP, to ask if he would set up an appointment for me, due to my illness. It didn't do me any harm, that much is obvious, but I don't know if it helped me or not. I thought 'in for a penny in for a pound'. Dr Reid referred me to the Homeopathic Hospital in London and Sophie and I used to drive down about once a month, to the top of Edgware Road tube station where we parked our van. We'd then take the tube into the centre of London.

The Homeopathic Hospital was part of the NHS, and I remember that it was a lovely old Victorian building, with beautiful architecture. Inside, it was very old fashioned, as was the homeopath I saw, quite an 'old dear' who was also a qualified medical doctor. She prescribed me a couple of tinctures. I don't know if they did me any good or not, really, but I was always well predisposed to homeopathy and I continued to go to the hospital in the hope that it could help. I was willing to try anything that might improve my chances of survival. I wasn't ready to give up the ghost yet.

In terms of mainstream medical treatment, I started on oral chemo tablets and a fairly high dose of steroids. That was all the medical profession could offer me as there was no other significant treatment for my type of cancer. I felt very puffy. Chemotherapy at the time didn't make me feel too bad – just a bit sick, so it wasn't the mad stuff you hear about which makes you wish you were dead anyway, apparently. I was given a fortnight on, then a fortnight off the steroids and chemo tablets, which went on like that for years.

I responded fairly well to the chemo and steroid tablets regime. I made sure that I ate healthily, had my five fruits and vegetables a day and I cut back on the alcohol.

I tried to live as healthily as possible, and worked on my fitness. I joined a proper gym and increased my gym work, including doing a proper weights programme. I met a chap there called Sean and we hung about together and did a lot of workouts at the gym..

My karate continued and I also continued to do sub-contractor work. When contracts came to an end, I would sign on the dole and claim the benefits I was entitled to. It was life as usual. What else can you do? When there's a mortgage and bills to pay, you just have to keep going. You've got to make a living. While you're living.

Talking of livers…

Sophie: Yeah. So you were taken off Cyclosporin, put on Tacrolimus, still on steroids, but somehow that really wasn't working either, and this graft-versus-host disease was just getting worse and worse, and affecting your liver at that time.

Norman: Yeah. That was my next question, to talk about the liver failure, the bilirubin.

Sophie: So yeah, so I can't really remember anybody ever sitting down and actually spelling out what was going on and what the sequence of events was, and what the matter actually was.

Norman: I can't remember any of this. I was going to college at that time.

Sophie: Yeah. And you were still going to karate as well, with
            me, at the university. Just really getting sicker and
            sicker, more and more jaundiced, and more and
            more like a patient with liver failure, actually; and that
            was through the autumn. So you became very, very
            jaundiced, and your bilirubin level was over 1,000.

Norman: What is it normally?

Sophie: It's normally under 30. It's 0-30 is the normal range.

Norman: Right. So I've got liver failure. I'm yellow.

Sophie: Yeah.

Norman: I remember somebody thinking that I was a
            Glaswegian Pakistani, I remember that. What is liver
            failure about, then? How does it show itself?

Sophie: Well, the main symptom, I suppose, that you get
            is jaundice. Your other symptoms depend on the
            reason why the liver failure is happening, but you had
            it because of damage to the liver bile ducts. So the
            graft-versus-host disease was attacking your liver bile
            ducts, so you couldn't get rid of your bilirubin really.
            And to make this diagnosis, you had to have a liver
            biopsy. Do you remember having that done?

Norman: No.

Sophie: No. Yeah. You had the first one done in Leicester.

Norman: Right.

Sophie: Down in the Radiology department. I remember you
             had that done by Dr Kim Kurup, who was lovely to
             you, actually. He let me come in and hold your hand,
             while he put in the local anaesthetic, and he talked
             you through it all. Lovely, lovely guy, and I ended
             up working with him in the end. He's since died: he
             died suddenly at 52. Had a sudden heart attack and
             dropped down dead. Just a lovely, lovely bloke and a
             real loss. So that was the first time I met Kim who did
             your liver biopsy, and he treated you very well. I was
             grateful to him for that.

             And they made the diagnosis that you'd got this
             thing called Vanishing Bile Duct Syndrome. They said
             that 90% of your bile ducts had been destroyed by
             graft-versus-host disease, you know, which clearly is
             only leaving you 10% to do what it needs to do. And
             so you did become very ill. Your liver wasn't working,
             and you had an accumulation of fluid in your belly,
             do you remember? Your belly was very distended.

Norman: No. The only thing I can remember is the…

Sophie: Itching.

Norman: … the itching.

Sophie: Yeah. So you lost a lot of weight, your skin became very papery, and

you smelled funny, because of all the things building up in your body. The bilirubin was building up in your body making you extraordinarily itchy, day and night. You had intractable itching underneath all of your skin because of the bile acids that were building up there, and it was just...

Norman: It was driving me mad.

Sophie: It was just intolerable, wasn't it?

Norman: It still stands out as probably the worst part of my treatment, really, the itch. No matter how hard I scratched, to the point that I was getting blood and skin under my nails, I couldn't get rid of it. And it's still one of the greatest horrors.

Sophie: Well, it was indescribably awful, wasn't it? Indescribably awful! And it went on for weeks, actually. They tried to give you different treatments for it: something called Ursodeoxycholic Acid, which was a powder and a tablet, and then you had that powder called Questran, which gave you diarrhoea. And it was around that time that the incident on Saffron Lane happened. I don't know if you wanted to mention that incident.

63

Norman: Yeah. I shat myself on the way home.

Sophie: So you do want to mention it. Yeah. That was around
            that time.

I would never use public loos, because I thought they were
horrible stinky places. Having a pee was alright but if I
needed a number two, then I wouldn't poo in a public
toilet because you didn't know what you were sitting on. I
remember going into Northampton one day with Sophie,
and we'd no sooner got there than I announced that I
needed to go home and attend to my toileting needs.

I tell you, my bowels seem to be the story of my life!
I think I've shat enough bricks over the years to build a
house. That was another thing that used to get on Sophie's
pip. I must add that I'm now so much better, because I
don't care now where I go for a dump. I just think "if it's
gonna' kill me, it's gonna' kill me!"

Chapter 5

Norman: I mean, that was when I was on plasma treatment.

Sophie: That's the same time, yeah. So they tried to give you these things to help with the itching, but they didn't help.

Norman: I went to Birmingham prior to the plasma.

Sophie: Yes. And you were given some sort of plasmapheresis, because your liver wasn't working properly, not producing any clotting factors. So they were giving you four units of fresh frozen plasma every day, which replaced all your clotting factors.

Norman: They couldn't get my bilirubin count down, so they referred me to Dr Mutimer in Birmingham, who stabilised everything and put me on plasma treatment, which was then carried on at Leicester for weeks and weeks. But whilst I was in Birmingham, I seem to remember that there was talk about a liver transplant in the pipeline.

Sophie: Yeah, you're right. I mean, it seemed things happened quite quickly, but by this time, early December, I suppose, you were so very sick, so very ill, do you remember, you were literally…

Norman: Dying.

Sophie: Yeah, dying. Your lips had frosted over as well, do you
            remember that? You were on a lot of steroids and
            your face was all puffy, and you really were not well.

            And Dr Hutchinson took me aside, and I think this
            was probably the first honest conversation that he
            had with me actually, and he said, "Do you realise
            how ill Norman is?"

            I said, "Well, yes, I realise he's very ill."

            And he said, "Well, yes, he is very ill."

            And I was like, "Oh, come on! Come out with it! So,
            you know, how long is he going to live for?"

            And he said, "Well, if things carry on as they are, he's
            going to live for a maximum of two weeks…" which
            was just awful, but he did come out and say it and he
            was honest. He said, "The only thing I think is going
            to help at this point will be a liver transplant, so we're
            trying to get him up to Birmingham to be assessed
            for this," and that was that!

            Looking back, you wonder how you get through
            these times, don't you? It is such a long time ago
            now, but you know, how do you get through that?
            Just in a state of numb disassociation, I suppose. It

just doesn't quite seem real, but you have to soldier through and get on with it. So...

Norman: For my part, it's just belligerence and just refusing to believe what people say a lot of the time, I suppose.

Sophie: Yeah, because it is kind of unreal, so there is a level on which you don't believe it, I guess. But the frustrating thing about this for me, was that, once somebody's told you that a liver transplant is the only thing and you have to go to Birmingham, the next thing you want to do is get in the car and drive to Birmingham. You would assume that under the circumstances, that is what would happen. But no, that is not what happened. What we had to do was wait for a bed to become available in Birmingham liver unit. And I can remember just ringing them up, ringing them up, and ringing them up, demanding, "When is this bed going to be available?"

"Well, it might be tomorrow..." "Well, it might be this afternoon..." "Well, it might be in the morning."

I was just constantly ringing. And there was a nice registrar, I can't remember what his name was, but I finally managed to make some sort of human contact with this nice registrar, who did keep ringing me, telling me what was going on, and keeping me informed. I could ring him at any time as well, which was great, because waiting for this bed was just awful.

You know, you shouldn't be having to wait two or three days for a bed, when you've got two weeks to live. It was… you probably don't even remember that, but it was just vile. And anyway…

Norman: I remember when we did finally get a bed that the ward was fucking awful.

Sophie: Oh, it was disastrous. I can remember being really, really anxious about having to drive you to hospital in Birmingham, because I don't think I was very confident about driving at that time. I was worried about finding the hospital in Birmingham City Centre. So I remember poring over maps, asking people, and trying to work out how to get there, because obviously you weren't in a fit state to be navigating, so I had to navigate and drive in a place that I'd never been to before. But bizarrely, the one thing I do remember about that trip, is that in reality, it was absolutely fine. It is the easiest journey in the entire world!

When we actually got to the hospital, the problem was trying to find somewhere where I could park the car, to get you out and walk you to the liver unit, because you were so frail. It was all barriered off, and there were lots of jobsworth car park attendants. You weren't allowed through the barriers, and the car park was fucking miles away. I was trying to explain to the car park attendants, getting them to poke their heads in and see that you really were not well, and could I please come through the barrier to park the car so I could let you out, to try and find this ward? And eventually, somebody must have taken pity on us, because we got you up to the ward. But do you remember, on the way to the ward, the hospital was falling apart? It was just beyond belief. Do you remember all of the windows were just sealed up with black and silver duct tape, because the windows were draughty or whatever.

Norman: Leaking.

Sophie: Leaking water. It just did not inspire confidence. And so... got you onto the ward and I was met by that nice registrar whose name I'm very, very sorry that I've forgotten, but, a nice guy. And that was a mixed ward, male and female. And they had those partitions in between every two beds. It was a Nightingale ward, and it was horrid. So they put you there, and obviously Dr Mutimer would have had a look at you. They did another liver biopsy. And there was lots of chuntering about liver transplants. At one point, you were on a step down ward for people who'd had liver transplants.

Norman: Yeah.

Sophie: Yeah. And this was all shortly before Christmas, and so they...

Norman: The nurses were horrible as well.

Sophie: The nurses were horrible, yeah. And they got you on
            this FFP. Four units of FFP every day, and I suppose
            you were getting better, or your blood results and
            things must have been getting better, but I'm not
            really sure if it was because…

Norman: They took me off the Tacrolimus.

Sophie: …they took you off the Tacrolimus. Yes, that's right.
            And you were just on steroids then, weren't you?

Norman: They spent weeks and weeks, after I got the start, you
            know, improving.

Sophie: Well, you were let out for Christmas.

Norman: I wasn't well.

Sophie: You didn't have a Hickman line then, because
            remember, they kept having to put cannulas in you?

Norman: Yeah.

Sophie: And there was a really nice house officer, with really
            long hair and a bum bag, and she used to come
            and put your cannulas in, and she was the only nice
            person working on the ward. She was lovely, and she
            told me where the staff fridge was, like, and showed

me I could put some food in the staff fridge for
you, because the food was appalling. And the nice
registrar let you out for Christmas, and Dan came
to get you. No. Yeah. Me and Dan, in Dan's Orion,
came to get you and we went to my mum's house
for Christmas Day, and she'd invited Joyce and Dave
and Sally down for Christmas, to stay, which was
nice of her. So we had that Christmas Day together,
managed to get back despite my brother's driving.

But you gradually got better, so you were discharged
as an outpatient, but you had to have four units of
fresh plasma every day. God knows how many units
of blood products you've had over the years.

Norman: And that was when I met...

Sophie: That was when you met Elaine and John.

Norman: Gamble. Elaine and John Gamble.

Sophie: Gamble, yes. Thought you said Campbell. You met
            them in the day room when you were going there
            every day for several hours' worth of this transfusion.
            You used to walk up. Yeah. You can't have... you
            must have been significantly better at that time, if
            you could walk up to the hospital and not have to
            drive.

Norman: You know what I'm like.

Sophie: Yeah. You had another Hickman line put in then,
             your second Hickman line, because your veins were
             all giving up, and they had to give you this every day.
             So you've had two Hickman lines, and the second
             one was for that fresh frozen plasma treatment. I
             don't know how many months it went on for, but
             it went on for a long time. And you met Elaine and
             John Gamble, and you gradually got better.

Norman: Was I still getting chest infections at this point?

Sophie: No, your lungs were okay at that point. You had
             a... after that, you had a period of relative quiet,
             I suppose, and you had your transplant in 95, so
             that would have been 96, coming into 96, when
             you started to get better, and things were relatively
             quiescent, I suppose.

Norman: I noticed this on the other sheet. What is reactive
             depression? It's nothing to do with this, but...

Sophie: It's depression that happens as a reaction to some
             sort of life event, like bereavement or, you know, job
             stress or... So it's not depression that just happens
             because your brain gets imbalanced. It happens
             because of an event, which leads the chemicals
             in your brain to become imbalanced and you get
             depressed.

Norman: Okay. I think the next thing I remember, or the next big thing, was probably my joint replacements. Can you talk about my two hips and my knee, tell me what that was all about? And when, basically? The left hip was done first.

Sophie: Yeah. I've been trying to think about when these things occurred, and I suppose you did have a period of relative good health, in that the graft-versus-host disease was quiescent, and you could breathe, and you were able to be fairly active, and resumed the things you enjoy doing, cycling, going to the gym, working, walking the dogs and things. But the main things that happened were that you had two hip replacements, a partial knee replacement and your cataracts. Did you forget about your cataracts?

Norman: Yeah, I've got that down.

Sophie: You've got that down. And I can't really remember which order they happened in actually.

Norman: My left hip...

Sophie: So, what happened with your left hip? I suppose the reason why you got early onset arthritis was because of your sporting activities and things, but also because the graft-versus-host disease affects your joints, and being on a very high dose of steroids can affect your hip joints, as well. And I suppose radiation isn't brilliant for your bones and joints. So, lots of reasons for you to have arthritis. You became increasingly troubled with pain in all of your joints, but mainly in your hips, to the point when, actually, you didn't want to do anything. You didn't want to go on holiday. You didn't want to go on walks. It really made you bloody miserable, I have to say.

It must have been very painful. And it caused you a lot of upset. You used to really be very upset and in pain… yeah, with your arthritis. It wasn't good at all. You didn't want to go out because they were hurting. Probably weren't sleeping that well. So I suppose you must have been referred at some point to Mr Power, the orthopaedic surgeon, who agreed that you could have a hip replacement.

Norman: What does that involve?

Sophie: So you had the first one done under general anaesthetic, and that was at the Glenfield. And what they do is, they make a cut, well, how long is your cut? Nine inch cut, down the side of your hip joint, and they go through all the layers, and then they basically cut off the end of your femur, and replace it with a big metal thing, which is the same shape as the end of a femur, with a big spike that goes down into the centre of the femur. They just hammer it in, quite literally. And then the cup part of the joint, which is in your pelvis, they drill that away, as well, and they replace that with a new metal cup part.

So it's a very big operation that you had done there, and obviously, it doesn't hurt afterwards because the two surfaces that are wearing on each other are no longer there. So the first hip replacement that you had was very good, and you were looked after fairly well on the ward, because you had got a button to press for pain: a PCAs button. You were in a bay next to a window, and you were reasonably well attended to. You had a catheter for a day or so until you were mobile, and then the physios got you out of bed, and you made a really good recovery after that. And I don't remember you having many complaints about things on that occasion. And you were walking with sticks when you came home, but...

Norman: I bounced back quite well.

Sophie: ...other than that, you were pretty good; you were okay.

Norman: Oh yeah, I would say so.

Sophie: And you had both hips done and then your knee.

Norman: Again, the nursing at one of them, I seem to remember asking to be catheterised because I was desperate to pee.

Sophie: That was the knee. So you had your other hip done after that, did you?

75

Norman: Mm mm.

Sophie: And again, Mr Power did your surgery and that went
            fine, but for some bizarre reason, they didn't give you
            a morphine pump after the operation, because they
            didn't have anybody that knew how to use them
            or something like that. So you had to keep asking
            for a morphine injection. But of course, you have to
            have two nurses to get that out of the controlled
            drugs cupboard to check it, and you have to find
            the keys… And two nurses on a busy ward, at two
            to four hourly intervals, it just wasn't happening. So
            I remember after the second hip replacement, you
            being in an awful lot of pain because of inadequate
            analgesia, because of nursing issues. And that was
            appalling actually, although you did have a side
            room. But the care the second time round really
            wasn't so good at all. And I can remember the
            physios coming to get you out of bed, and you
            hadn't had any pain relief, so that was an issue with
            your second hip replacement. But nevertheless, you
            got out of hospital, and that's when Elaine came to
            collect you, because I was not able to come, and
            somebody came and told you that your wife had
            come to collect you, and you were expecting to see
            me, but it was Elaine. So that was your second hip
            replacement.

I've always been active. Always worked laboriously.
Always relied on my physical strength and skills. And my

hips.

It seemed as though I'd only been down in Northampton for five minutes when I got a job with this company called CHA – a communications and computer networking company. I can't remember how old I was when I got a job with CHA – probably about 24years old. Basically I was running big cables and connecting them up. We did big jobs. We worked in Whitehall, putting computers in there and also in Guinness Headquarters, and Barclays Headquarters. They were huge, big jobs, and it was great work. By this time, Trevor and I had bought a house together because we were both fed-up of paying for digs, basically. Trevor was still working as an electrician but with a different company from me. Everything in the garden was coming up roses! I was getting well paid at CHA, there was lots of overtime and I got the use of a company car. The only drawback about working for CHA was that Sam, my dog, had to go into kennels every time I worked away from home. Sam was so good in kennels that the kennel owners used to have him in their home: they loved Samson. He was so well behaved after all his training.

I loved the job. The hourly rate wasn't brilliant but you got paid for your traveling time at full whack and as much overtime as you wanted. You also got to use the works van and although I paid for the diesel I used privately, you could have put it on the card. Honest, me, eh?! The job took us all over the country. We got proper digs when we were away from home. The working week was so long that we were getting paid sixty or seventy hours a week.

I was chuffed to bits with it! CHA are based in Milton Keynes. I drove the thirty miles from Wellingborough to Milton Keynes every morning. I was an engineer there – that was my title. We also had an engineer's assistant who did all the fetching and carrying for you. Because of my outspoken views and belligerence, myself and another guy called Alan Flounder, who was equally outspoken and belligerent, were put together to work as a team. We got on like a house on fire! He had his own car and didn't want the works van so I got it to use as my own – brilliant! After some time, we got paid off . Our payoff was given for 2 years 11 months - to give us 3 years' redundancy would have cost the company too much money. Tight gits! I went to work for a contractor at Weetabix by the name of Pat Waller, and Alan went to work for a fire alarm company.

Pat Waller was pretty well off. He came to own a nice old folks home, run by his wife that by chance, Sophie's granny ended up at. He, meanwhile, had this electrical contracting business. Weetabix had a nice canteen that overlooked the river which was lovely. I managed to save up a bit of money which would keep me going through the drought, as it were. Pat paid well over the odds, and I used to get loads of overtime from him. I'd be working 6, 8 or 12 hour days per week and this could go on for 1, 2 or 3 months and so I'd accumulate all this money and have no time to spend it. So from that point of view, it was good. Now, Pat was a man of very few words and when he did speak he was generally grumpy, so me and him got on just fine. He didn't like Trevor for whatever reason. I don't know why, because Trevor worked as hard as anybody.

I remember when Sophie and I were doing up our first house in Sheridan Street in Leicester. Again, my pal Graham did a lot of the work and we'd bought this real-flame effect gas fire, which was a sort of mock Victorian thing. When the house was done, we put it on, but the fire was rubbish as it wouldn't give out any heat! So we went back to the shop we bought it from and complained about it. The owner said, "Aw, no. They are just meant to look good – they're not meant to give out heat."

We don't know if he was telling the truth, but we were young and a bit naïve so we didn't really want to argue about it. So we had this decorative fire that gave out decorative flames, but less heat than a candle. We fitted new windows and Sophie and I did the painting and decorating. Sophie organised the plants, hanging baskets, herbs and so on. In order to have our home looking the way we wanted it to look, we even worked on Christmas Day 1994!

Sophie and the power tool incident occurred when we were in the finishing stages of doing the house up in Sheridan Street, around about our wedding time. Graham was doing the plastering work and we had this big electric drill with a large paddle attached, to mix the plaster up. Sophie asked Graham if she could have a shot of this drill. Well, I don't know what happened but she managed to get the drill jammed. The paddle wasn't moving but the bucket was spinning round and round. The bucket was also winding the cable around itself, so the cable was getting shorter and shorter. Sophie being Sophie, instead of calmly switching the drill off, she just let the drill go. The drill kept running, the bucket was bouncing about and all this plaster was jumping out all over the place. Me and Graham couldn't do anything for falling about the floor, laughing at Sophie. It was really quite funny. Sophie was covered from head to toe in wet plaster and so were the windows, the walls and the ceiling.

While I was at Weetabix my mum died and I approached Pat and told him my mum had passed away. He was very sympathetic and said, "Oh, I suppose you'll be wanting time off for the fuckin' funeral, next!"

I replied, "That's very kind of you Pat, thank you."

I remember as my illness got worse, all these lumps on my head started to appear. I was quite drained and tired; the long shifts at work were taking their toll on me and I was becoming slower and slower at my work. One day, Pat lost it and blatantly told me I was lazy and useless. So I walked off site, seething, went home and picked up the letter I'd recently received from the hospital telling me what these lumps were. I took it back to Pat and thrust it at him. He read it and gave it back to me, in silence. I took the letter back, irritated and disappointed in him, and went home. He rang up and apologised, which was amazing, as it was quite unheard of for Pat to ever apologise.

I think soon after, I left the job, because whilst I wouldn't like to admit to feeling dreadful and finding the work too hard to manage, I think that was the reality.

Post-transplant, but prior to liver failure, I was a bit restless after coming out of hospital and got a job as a barman part-time in the Saffron Working Men's Club. It was a bit of a shithole and some bastard stole my car and fucked it up. Still, the insurance paid for it, so you just have to shrug your shoulders and accept that shit happens. It's just that I must have been standing right in front of the fan whenever shit hit it. Then my liver failure kicked in big time and my jaundice set in, making my skin increasingly yellow. So I had to leave: my colour was scaring the customers away! They didn't know if what I had was catching – fucking thick working men's club drinkers were ignorant of jaundice and thought it was contagious. It wasn't even as if they were afraid I was an advert for the dangers of drink! So they carried on developing cirrhosis, still knocking back the beers, while driving me out of another job.

If illness doesn't bring you to your knees, other people can.

Sophie: Then you did definitely, for sure, have your knee replacement in 2000. It's crazy when you think back, all this, isn't it? So I was working nights for a week on a labour ward. How many dogs did we have then? Four? You were in hospital for a week, but I was kind of coping. Don't ask me how, because I don't know.

But I can remember speaking to the sister in charge and saying, "I work here and I'm working nights, so obviously, I'm not going to be able to get here during visiting times to see Norman during the daytime, but would it be alright, if my shift isn't too busy, if I come and see him some time before 10 o'clock?" and they said, yes, under the circumstances, that would be absolutely okay.

So I can remember the day you had your operation, wandering up to see you on the orthopaedic ward at the General, in my scrubs, with my theatre shoes on, feeling a bit tired because I was on nights. And when I got there, you were okay but you hadn't peed since the operation, bearing in mind this would have been after 8 o'clock.

Norman: So how long had I...? Why did I...? Because again, I sort of remember being desperate to pee.

Sophie: Yes. Yeah, well, you would have been, because even if you'd come out of theatre at the very latest at 5.00, they'd have filled you up with a load of fluid in theatre, and you wouldn't have had a pee for three hours at the very least. And I suspect it was probably a lot, lot longer than that.

Norman: I remember crying that night in pain.

Sophie: Yes. Well, urinary retention is extraordinarily painful. But it's because of the anaesthetic drugs that your bladder doesn't work. So they'd called somebody to come and do a catheter, because at that time, female nurses weren't allowed to catheterise male patients. But whoever was coming was obviously tied up somewhere else, and we kind of briefly floated the idea of me doing it for you, but the ward nurses were not happy about that at all, you know, quite rightly, because that's not... it isn't really appropriate.

Norman: It wasn't appropriate, but nobody else was doing it.

Sophie: No. I appreciate that. I completely understand where you're coming from, but, you know, I felt quite uncomfortable about it. They were not having it. So, on balance, I thought it was probably best that this person wouldn't be too long. So eventually you did get your catheter. The other thing...

Norman: Yeah, I think he came at 11 o'clock and did it.

Sophie: The other thing that you were unhappy about, about your knee replacement was, they'd made you have it done under spinal. Do you remember?

Norman: I remember I was awake.

Sophie: Yeah. I think you might have had a bit of cough or cold or something, or, I don't know, the anaesthetist was just in a bad mood or something, but they'd said that unless you had it done under spinal, they wouldn't do it. They wouldn't anaesthetise you, so of course, you had to agree, and... I mean, I don't know what that experience was like.

Norman: I can't remember.

Sophie: You can't remember. But you weren't very happy that they hadn't let you have a general anaesthetic.

Norman: So basically, I was numb from the bum down.

Sophie: Yeah.

Norman: But aware of what was going on.

Sophie: Yeah. And couldn't pee because of the drugs, the spinal anaesthetic drugs. And that wouldn't happen now, you know. I mean, certainly, in obstetrics, anybody that gets a spinal for whatever, gets a catheter at the same time until the next day, because, you know, they recognise that that's the right thing to do. I don't know what happens in orthopaedics, but anyway. So you did make a good recovery from that, and you were home within a few days, came home to Avebury Avenue. You'd had arthroscopies before that.

Norman: Cleanouts.

Sophie: Cleanouts, yes. And yes, you'd arranged to have an arthroscopy around the time we were moving, hadn't you? Yes, in fact, I'll tell you, you were in hospital having an arthroscopy on the day we moved from Sheridan Street to Avebury Avenue..

Norman: Yeah. I remember coming home and the removals
            men were there.

Sophie: Yeah, you weren't there. I'd had to soldier on, on my
            own again, with the dogs and everything. Anyway, it
            was fine. I got moved.

Norman: We got moved.

Sophie: Yeah, we got moved. But you were in hospital having
            an arthroscopy that day.

Chapter 6

My granny Mac died. I don't think I was at work at the time due to my illness and I didn't have a vehicle to get up to Scotland for her funeral. My granny's daughter Auntie Wilma and Uncle Jim said if I could get myself to Chester, they would give me a lift up. That was still going to be a bit of a problem, but not insurmountable. I asked Trev if I could borrow his car, without really thinking. He said that was ok, so I was sorted. If you can call it that. Stitched up might be a better description, but I did it myself.

Now, a bit of background on Trev and cars. He's never spent any more than £300 on a car, ever – even to this day. So whenever the car he was driving broke down (which they did with regular monotony) Trevor just left them, and walked away. He'd take his stuff out of the car and hitch home. So I borrowed his Datsun – and that tells you how old it was, pre-Nissan – a big old car, and totally rusty. The bonnet was so rusty that it looked like the ripped edge of a tin can; the panels were all different colours and I don't suppose it was even road taxed. I foolishly took the car.

When I was driving along and looked out of the back window, I could see nothing for the clouds of blue smoke as I chugged along. I could have hired it out as a smoke machine for rock concerts, if only the sound of the engine hadn't been louder than any heavy metal rock band. I left the motorway, relieved that I hadn't met any police, and was just approaching Nantwich when I heard a *Nee*

86

naw! *Nee naw!* – the unmistakable sound of a police siren, although I couldn't see any flashing lights. The police drew up alongside me and indicated for me to pull over, which I did at the next lay-by.

The policeman said, "Didn't you see us?"

I said, "No, I could hear you, but I couldn't see you for all the smoke."

"Is this car yours?" The police asked me.

"You must be joking! I wouldn't be seen dead in a thing like this!" I laughed, blatantly alive in the thing, and clearly being seen. "But I've got to get to Chester, because it's my granny's funeral and the only way I can get to Chester is in this banger which belongs to my mate!"

The policeman said, "Well, it's not taxed."

I said, "I know that, but I'm not taxing it myself for just a couple of days. I wouldn't normally be in it, but I just need to get to Chester, to get a lift up to Scotland for my gran's funeral!"

The policeman was really nice while at the same time pointing out all the problems with the car. He said he would give me a seven day ticket and within that time period I'd to get the car taxed and MOT'd and the arches of the car repaired.

He said, "If you don't do that, then you've got to scrap the car and send me proof of the scrapping from the scrap yard, otherwise we'll come after you."

I said, "Well, that's decent of you, thanks!"

So I got to my gran's funeral, and back to Chester to pick up Trev's car with 3 days still left on the 7 day ticket. I explained to Trev what happened and he went and got the car taxed, and between the pair of us we got a sheet of steel that we riveted onto the good bits of the wings, bending them over the rusty stuff, pop-riveted it again and took it to a garage to see if it was roadworthy. I tell you this, it was a fuckin' mess. It was a green and yellow car where Trevor had painted and repaired it with big patches of steel plate that had been riveted along the bonnet and along the wheel arches. Anyway, the guy at the garage said, "Yeah, that's safe enough" and passed it!

We roared and laughed. Trevor always had crap cars and he was always doing stupid stuff with them. He landed the nickname "Trevor Fuckwit" because of his daft antics.

If you didn't keep your eye on him, anything could happen.

Norman: The next thing is the cataracts. Again, how the symptoms manifested themselves.

Sophie: The cataracts, I really can't remember when you had those done. Was it 98, end of 98? It was, wasn't it? Because you were having problems with cataracts when we lived in Sheridan Street, because I remember you couldn't go out. You couldn't, you really couldn't see. And the reason again...

Norman: I was using a magnifying glass to read stuff.

Sophie: Yeah. The reason, again, for having the cataracts was for sure to do with the treatment that you'd received, in terms of the radiation and the high dose steroids. Both of those things give you cataracts. And, of course, none of these things were explained to you prior to having this, but, I suppose, they thought that all they had to tell you is, if you didn't have it, you'd be dead. So yeah, that must have been around 98, Norman...

Norman: And so we were worried about blindness.

Sophie: So yes, that manifested itself with blindness really, which was insidious, and it got worse fairly quickly actually, to the point where really, for quite a long time, you were housebound. You were using a magnifying glass to read, and tried to struggle on in college, but it did get to the point where you didn't feel confident outside the house. You certainly couldn't drive, and you didn't feel confident about crossing the road. Do you remember that?

Norman: No.

Sophie: No, you couldn't cross the road unaided. And it did get very, very bad. Liz Bibby was pretty good though, your ophthalmologist, she managed to squeeze you in, didn't she, to have at least one done. And you had...

Norman: I remember crying when I came round, and the bandages were taken off.

Sophie: Well, you weren't supposed to peep, were you,
            underneath the bandage, but I think you did peep.
            But yes, did you have that done under general or
            under local?

Norman: General. I cried.

Sophie: Yes.

Norman: I was so pleased to see again.

Sophie: So grateful and so pleased that you could see. But
            that was very, very disabling. So you had one done.
            I think she squeezed you in for the first one, so at
            least you could see and read and be mobile and be
            independent, but you had to wait a fair time to have
            the second one done. But it didn't matter so much
            because at least you'd got sight in one eye.

Norman: And that was when she left a thread, a stitch.

Sophie: The second one? Yeah, that's right. So that would
            have been…

Norman: When we went to Orkney.

Sophie: When did we go to Orkney?

Norman: It was in the Volvo.

Sophie: In the Volvo. When were the puppies born? 97.

Norman: Think so.

Sophie: Think so. This would have all been 97, you know, I think. I think so.

Norman: Yeah. She left a stitch in.

Sophie: Yes. Well, whoever had done your surgery had left you stitched a bit too long. Because the first operation, cataract operation, was fine, wasn't it. And the second one, the stitch had been left a little bit too long and it was like constantly having a bit of grit in your eye. Every time you blinked you could feel it.

Norman: It was driving me mad. It was quite sore actually in the end.

Sophie: Yeah. And so you struggled through a wet, cold holiday in Orkney in August, with that thing in your eye.

Norman: Yeah.

Sophie: Which wasn't making you best pleased.

Norman: No.

Sophie: No. Until we could get back. Because I think you

must have had it done, and then we must have gone to Orkney pretty much straight away after, because… a couple of days later, it became apparent that it just wasn't settling. And yeah, I think the first thing we did when we got back from Orkney, was go to eye casualty or something, wasn't it, and they said, oh, that's because the stitch has been left too long. And they trimmed it, didn't they?

Norman: Mm.

Sophie: And it was fine, instant relief.

November '92, I walked into the 3 horseshoes pub in Wellingborough and first laid eyes on Sophie who was working behind the bar. I thought she was lovely. Her hair was piled up on top of her head and she just looked stunning. More of Sophie later. I'll give you an intro into how this all came about.

In November '92, the interest rates were phenomenal. They were about 15%. As a result, Trevor and I were forced really to take in a couple of lodgers. Trevor was working away from home in Sudbury in Suffolk at the Lucas Electronics Plant, or somewhere in Didcot Power Station in Oxfordshire. So we had a couple of lodgers: Davie Smith who was Scottish, an ex-paratrooper, and about five feet tall. He was as wide as he was tall and a lovely guy. I liked Davie. The other chap was a guy called Phil but we just named him Mr Odd because he was very odd! I think he was an alcoholic but he was a dirty bastard as well. He used to shit all over the toilet pan – aw, he was horrible. So anyway, me, Davie and Trevor if he was home, would get a "shit, shave and shampoo" and we would go into the town. Now the route was a well-worn route, by me at any rate. We would all start off in the Coach and Horses with a few games of pool and a few beers, then into the White Swan which was called the "Quivering Quim" for reasons best known to the landlady! Allegedly, she would shag anybody – I don't know if that was true – I never went there!

After the White Swan, it was the Golden Hind and then the Three Horseshoes. As I say, I walked in there and Sophie caught my eye and immediately I was smitten. I never spoke to her, other than to ask her for a drink. I saw her a couple of days later in town, too – I think she was buying fireworks so it must have been the beginning of November.

The following Saturday I got very drunk. They were selling poppies everywhere, so it must have been around Armistice time. As I say, I got very drunk and Sophie was selling poppies. Sophie sold me a poppy, which I said I'd buy on the condition that she would pin it to my manly chest! So I got chatting to her. She seemed really nice and she had a lovely accent. So, I worked up courage to ask her out.

Although maybe it wasn't quite so romantic a start as Sophie thought. Being a man's man and all, it didn't really follow that course of true romance at that stage. Prior to that, I'd been discussing with Davie and Trevor the size of Sophie's boobs, when this woman, who'd overheard the conversation told me, "Don't be so pathetic! If you like the girl, ask her out!"

So I duly did. After a few drinks to pluck up the courage, of course. I asked Sophie out, but I had to fight off stiff competition in the form of the AA man. Sophie accepted my invitation of a date, despite me being pissed. She later told me that she went out with me rather than the AA man because I had asked her personally, whereas the AA man got his mate to do it. A bit like: "My mate fancies you. Will you go out with my friend?" like you did at school. Obviously a sad case! So that was that, and I was delighted. I never did like the AA.

I arranged to meet Sophie in the Three Horseshoes pub at 8 o'clock – it was during the week. Come eight thirty, there was no sign of Sophie, so I was convinced I'd been stood up. I was just about to finish my drink and go home to lick my wounds when she appeared. She apologised profusely saying she had been trying to control her two unruly brothers who had been throwing pasta up to the ceiling to see if it would stick. This apparently tells you if the pasta's cooked. I'd imagine it would also leave a hell of a mess on your ceiling! So she apologised for being late and we decided to get away from the Three Horseshoes pub where she worked, where there were lots of prying eyes, and went to a pub nearby, called The Sun. It was a quiet little pub and we chatted away.

She came across very quickly as being intelligent. She was sharp, level headed, and good looking. She told me about her two jobs, so she was hard working. She looked after her gran and two brothers while her parents were still in New Zealand. She clearly loved her gran and her two brothers and sounded very kind to them. She liked animals, the same music as me and we liked to go for walks. So all in all it was pretty good and I thought we had a good first date. My only concern was that she was only nineteen, and I was twenty-eight. She looked like twenty-two and I don't say that in a mean way. She just came across as very mature so I didn't really hold out much hope that she would want to continue seeing somebody nine years older than her. We agreed to meet again.

My second date with Sophie was going to the cinema in Wellingborough, to see 'The Fugitive' with Harrison Ford, I believe. It was in one of those old fashioned cinemas – an Art Deco type – the kind you just don't get any more, or if you do, they've been converted into bingo halls for the scuzzers. So, we had our second date in the Wellingborough cinema to see The Fugitive.

In time, I met Sophie's brothers, Keith and Dan, and her nan. One dinnertime her nan tried to poison me by putting two spoonfuls of salt in my tea! Her brother Dan told her that if I ever wore Old Spice aftershave she was to ditch me because only dirty old men wore Old spice aftershave! Was that good advice? I don't know! When her parents came back from New Zealand I met them and I must admit, I liked her mum from the off. It would be fair to say that I was not Sophie's stepfather Steve's favourite person, and to be fair he wasn't really my favourite person either. Our mutual dislike eventually made moving on with Sophie easier, in a lot of ways.

Sophie and I went out on long walks of a weekend,

Sundays usually. We used to go to Finedon Quarry which is an old disused iron stone quarry or Dig Woods just near Althorpe House. Sometimes we used to walk out by Burton Latimar, down past a farm and onto what looked like an old mill pond. On that particular walk Samson was bounding through the oilseed rape field and had to jump up every so often to get his bearings. That was quite funny. He was completely yellow by the time he came out of the field, his coat covered in pollen off the rapeseed. That was a good day and sticks in my mind.

Norman: Yeah. Talking about holidays and whatnot, what happened in Culloden Moor when my Hickman site erupted?

Sophie: Yeah, let me just turn this off for a sec because I need to get a drink.

            … holding music plays …

            Yes, Culloden Moor. I'm supposing this was when we'd been on holiday to the west coast. Is Culloden the west coast?

Norman: No, it's Inverness.

Sophie: Inverness, oh. But we'd driven up to Loch Ness to Inverness. So that was the year that we went to…

Norman: In the trusty Volvo.

Sophie: … in the trusty Volvo, we went to see Michael, wasn't it?

Norman: Stayed at Michael's.

Sophie: And that, I suppose, must have been because you'd not long had the Hickman line out, that must have been 1996, mustn't it?

Norman: Yeah.

Sophie: Mustn't it? Because that was summer, so that shows you how long that FFP treatment went on for.

Norman: It went on for four months.

Sophie: Well, I think it must have been longer than that. Because it was a summer holiday, and you'd not long had the Hickman line out. You didn't need it anymore, because your FFP treatment was over. And, of course, again, we'd gaily gone off up the road on the holiday, and you felt absolutely fine, didn't you? You hadn't had any pain in your chest or anything whatsoever; not really noticed anything wrong. And then we're out on the very first reach of Culloden Moor, and you said, oh, my tee-shirt's wet…

Norman: Dribble.

Sophie: …dribble on your chest, and your tee-shirt was wet.

You hadn't even felt it, which was a bit disturbing.
So we had a look, and you'd got this huge abscess
cavity in your chest where the Hickman line tunnel
had been, and it had just burst, and there was pus
everywhere. It was a huge abscess, it really was big.
And I can remember milking it out of the tunnel,
pushing it down, but we'd got no tissue. We hadn't
got a wet wipe or even got a scarf to wipe it up with.

Norman: It was loads.

Sophie: And there was loads of it, and it was all over the
place. So I think what you did, was you took your
tee-shirt off and you used that to wipe up the pus.
And there was a real dent where the pus had been.

Norman: Still is.

Sophie: Just like the dents that are still in your head, where
the lymphoma has eroded your skull. So we went
straight to the A&E in Inverness Hospital, didn't we?
And they had a look at you, and I supposed they
weren't concerned because at least the abscess had
drained itself, but they gave you some Flucloxacillin
to take, some oral antibiotics, which you did, and
some dressings, and…

Norman: Phone up?

Sophie: Well, no, I rang the bone marrow unit, actually, as well. Well, it's infection, isn't it? And they were paranoid about infection, so I thought I'd better just ring them up and run this past them, to make sure they didn't want you up in hospital for IV antibiotics, but they said no, that would be okay, thank goodness. And it continued to drain pus, despite the antibiotics, and I think I must have taken you into the bone marrow unit when we got back, because Phil Murphy had a look at you, and he said, 'Oh, well, what's happened is the cuff of the Hickman line has been left behind, the cuff that holds it inside, under the skin, and that's why it's become infected.'

I don't know whether he could feel it or what, I can't remember, but he was sure it was there. And I can remember he'd cut into the abscess cavity to try and retrieve the cuff, but he couldn't. And you had to be referred to plastic surgery. Remember that?

Norman: No.

Sophie: No. Well, you did. You had to be referred to plastic surgery, so Mr Millward looked after you; he's a nice guy as well, he's retired now. I think you had a GA for it, and they did it on their day case list. They had to open up the track of the Hickman Line, where it was tunnelled under your skin, by about, what, three inches?

Norman: Correct.

Sophie: That's how long your scar is, isn't it? And they retrieved the cuff from inside, that was causing the abscess, and I suppose they gave it a good old clean out and debrided it and everything. And they sewed it up, and they obviously made it very, very neat, being plastic surgeons, and that was that little episode over. But again, frankly, you could have done without the Hickman line cuff being left inside, or at the very least, the person that took it out…

Norman: Should have noticed there was a bit missing.

Sophie: Yeah, but there we go.

Chapter 7

The same year I met Sophie, 1992, my mum died and by the time everything got done and dusted I think my sisters and I were left about £1300 each. Not a great deal of money, given the fact that my mum lived to be in her sixties. However, she was widowed at 52 years old and had to look after herself and her family on her earnings from a part time job. She lived in a council house and the stuff in it wasn't worth a great deal. My share of Mum's money bought me a holiday with Trev in USA. This is what my Mum should have done, treated herself. She had this £4,500 but she would never have spent it on herself, she just had it kept away for a rainy day and of course, the poor old dear died and the rainy day when she needed to spend it never came. Interestingly, she was never in debt and her funeral was totally paid for through her insurance. So I went on holiday to America with Trev to visit his uncle in San Francisco and it just being the way it is with the family's ages, Trev's uncle Allan was the same age as Trev. Allan was a nice chap, in IT, married to a Filipino training to be a dentist. He had gone over to America and done really well for himself – and they are doing even better for themselves now that his wife has qualified as a dentist!

Part of my and Trevor's travel deal to the USA was a free night in an airport hotel prior to our morning flight to America, and that all went very well. When we went down for breakfast Trevor ate baked beans, fried eggs, hash browns, and as much as he could get on his plate. Then the bus took us to Heathrow, where we checked in and boarded our plane. The cabin staff were serving drinks one after the other, and at this time smoking was still permitted on the plane. There was a permanent blue haze of smoke, me getting steadily drunker and Trevor producing the aromatic results of his fried breakfast from his arse – he was smoking from both ends and stinking! He thought it was dead funny because he was immune to the smell and he farted most of the way to America: a real tail wind!

When we were in America, Trevor's Uncle Allan took us to Nevada for two or three nights' gambling at the Circus Hotel. Trevor enjoys a gamble, although I'm not a great fan of it. My money has always been too hard to come by to just throw it away! I spent a bit of time wandering around the place – these Casinos are huge! You don't necessarily have to play the machines, you can just go and be entertained by people-watching. But Trev, the one-legged man, started on the one-armed bandits.

Anyway, I'd decided my limit was going to be twenty dollars, so I got this big tub of quarters and started to play the one-armed bandit. I quickly sussed that if you were playing the one-armed bandit, the waitresses would come round and serve you free beer. Obviously, if you weren't playing, you weren't offered a drink. So I used to keep my eye out, spot the waitress coming and then start playing the machine and so got free beer all night. At the end of the night I landed a hundred dollar jack-pot! Great! It was

a cheap night. I came away with eighty-five dollars, and
pissed! Trevor had managed to lose all his money at the
Pontoon and Black Jack tables – he had to get more money
wired in to him from Britain. Quite funny. Typical Trevor!
Although, because he was playing the tables he got spirits
instead of beer – but that obviously didn't do him much
good!

I liked the US in parts. You can get huge tubs of ice
cream for a few dollars, and when I say huge, I'm talking
two-pint tubs for only two or three dollars. So, Trevor
and I used to grab a spoon from Allan's kitchen, walk
down to the supermarket and buy a tub of ice cream and
just walk home, sit on the wall and stuff our faces. It was
marvellous. Budweiser was only a shiver a bottle, too – it
cost you more to piss, I think.

What I didn't like about America was the abject
poverty – so obvious on the streets, with people sleeping
in doorways. For such a wealthy country, it's a dog-eat-dog
world and people are all for themselves.

We went to New Orleans when we were in America,
just after Mardi Gras, and landed in New Orleans airport,
which is about 20 miles from New Orleans, at about
3am. Of course, there were no buses running, so our first
expense was a taxi. We asked to be dropped off somewhere
we could get a hotel, and the taxi driver dropped us in the
shittiest district. All the hotels had winos sitting drinking
in the foyer, with the man on reception with a fag in his
mouth, sitting just in his grubby vest, watching telly.
Well, it was that kind of district, so we basically panicked,
saying to ourselves, "Fuck's sake! We're going to get

mugged!" because here we are, trailing along the streets with our suitcases behind us.

We finally found ourselves safely in the French Quarter and booked into the Dauphin Hotel, which was lovely. But unfortunately, it was a four star hotel which took up most of our money to book in for the five days, so we had to be very careful what we spent our money on. We paid upfront so there was no fear of being kicked out in the street. New Orleans is a strange place, again full of beggars and young, black, male prostitutes. When I say young, I'm talking about 10 or 12 years old, offering you sexual favours. It was a bit sad, really. The bars were full of Jazz and Blues players and they were really good but all a bit seedy. When you looked around the corners, you could see a lot of drug activity and all that jazz...!

New Orleans felt a bit scary if you went out of the French Quarter. Although maybe not now, because since the floods it's been washed away, of course. I remember there was a bit of a scuffle involving a couple of black guys and the police were roughing them up a bit. It caught my attention and I started taking photos, but of course, that drew the attention of the police. They came up to me and roughed me up a bit, took my spool of film out of the camera, handed me the camera back and called me a "Mo'fo" a number of times. Motherfucker! I told them I was British and that he couldn't speak to me like that, to which he replied: "Mo'fo!"

I went on an old river boat up the Mississippi, too. And saw Napoleon's death mask – well, that's what it said – it might have been a cheap forgery!

After New Orleans we went off back to Nevada and met Trev's uncle Allan and Mair, and booked into the Circus Hotel – a huge place. So big, it's got a circus in it, in fact, resplendent with trapeze artists and anything else circusy; but no animals, I'd like to add.

No wonder so many Americans are obese. Let me give you an example of over the top eating – in our hotel there were no plates for your breakfast: you got a huge plastic tray with indentations which you basically filled up with everything your heart desired. Every hole was filled by the Americans, so they ended up with a mountain of food. They would scoff it all and go back for more. So it's no surprise they put on weight, and also no wonder there are people starving, because the waste was just phenomenal, too. They ought to be ashamed of themselves, actually.

Just had to get that off my chest.

Norman: What happened then?

Sophie: Well, I'll tell you about the bit before, because that was interesting. But you were being treated at home for a chest infection, and you'd given a sputum sample or something like that, and we'd had a call from the bone marrow unit to say they'd had your sputum results back. This was December 13, in the day. And they'd said that you'd got a fungal infection, in addition to the bacterial infection, and could I go in and pick up some different tablets for you to take as well as the Tazocin, to treat Candida, because you'd got Candida in your lungs. So that was that. So you started taking those, and then 2 o'clock in the morning, or whenever it was, I can't even remember, you started yelling at me and fortunately, I managed to wake up and go in and see what the matter was. You were out of bed, pacing around, couldn't breathe, very, very agitated, not really making sense, a bit confused. And you'd managed to make your way into the bathroom and sit on the loo, because you needed to go to the toilet.

Norman: I felt as though I needed to poo.

Sophie: Yeah, have your bowels open.

Norman: I'm not really house-trained at all.

I got Samson because I was scared I would just languish in my bed and start to feel sorry for myself if I wasn't careful. So I thought if I got a dog, I'd have to get up and about for the sake of the dog. I'd always fancied a German Shepherd dog or an Alsation, and there was an advert in the local paper for some puppies.

I went to see the pups, just outside Northampton. One of the puppies started chewing my laces and I thought, "He seems to have a bit of character about him", so I paid the woman the princely sum of £250 and came away with a chunky puppy. I called him Samson, because I thought he would probably grow up to be big and hairy, since he was from long-haired stock! Everyone told me that was a horse's name, but anyway, over time his name was shortened to Sam.

I took Sam to obedience training for dogs on a Tuesday night, where we'd go through all the basic things like: Sit! Stop! Start! Wait! Up! Down! Round! We were supposed to go away and practice all that during the week, so that when we returned to training the following Tuesday it would all have started to sink in! I wasn't working at that time due to ill-health, pre-transplant, so I used to train Sam for about two hours every day, going through the various drills with him. Because it's solitary and quite intense, I used to break up Sam's training, and every fifteen minutes or so we'd stop, and I'd take him for a walk or play and throw a stick or a ball for him. We did a lot of training every day and by the end of the training course, he was a super dog. He was such a delight to take out! He was never in any bother, and I was so glad that Sam and I put the effort in together.

Samson enjoyed yoghurt and whenever I was having some I used to give him the pot to lick out. Samson used to come everywhere with me and when Sophie stayed in Halls of Residence in her first year at University, I used to take Sam up when I went to see her and all the girls there used to feed him no end of stuff out of their fridge. He used to endear himself to people, but then he was good at that. They asked me what titbits Sam liked for preference. I answered 'yoghurt' and from then on the girls would feed Sam tubs of yoghurt and they knew him as 'yoghurt dog'!

Samson came everywhere with me and I remember once going down Abingdon Road in Northampton. It was a sunny day so the windows in the van were all down and Samson was in the back of the van. The van didn't have a backboard which meant that Samson could come and go between the front and the back of the van if he so pleased. I was stationary at traffic lights and this traffic cop had noticed that my tax disc was missing. Well, it wasn't actually missing: it was just one of those crappy plastic sticky holders that had lost its stickiness and had fallen off. Anyway, the cop stuck his head in the window of my van and started to berate me for not displaying my tax disc. Samson launched himself from the back of the van and 'woofed' loudly right in his ear. The traffic cop straightened up immediately in his hurry to escape and cracked his head on the top of the door. Aw, God, I tell you what – I tried really hard not to piss myself laughing. He shat himself! He was going to give me a ticket for not displaying my tax disc but he relented. He was a bit of a wanker. Samson could obviously tell.

When we lived in Avesbury Avenue, the shops were about ten minutes away. I took Samson out to walk to the shops for a few bits and bobs and on the way back my dog decided to have a crap outside the church gate at the same time as the wedding party was coming out. So there's me holding a taut lead, at the other end of which is my dog having a shit and the wedding party looking aghast. Of course, I didn't have any dog poo bags with me either, so I felt like a right minger: a dirty git, having to leave the steaming pile there for the wedding photos. I couldn't have been more humiliated if the wedding party had seen me creep into the crypt and crap, myself. Of course I think the dog thought it was really funny, but was

I embarrassed?!

That's the kind of things dogs do to you. No etiquette. No shame.

Samson used to love swimming, and when we were in Scotland we often used to go up to the River Almond which flowed towards Perth, to a place called Almondbank, because there was a nice level walk along there and a calm part before the river hit a small weir. Of course my old dog Samson was getting on by this point, and Samson got dragged into the weir. My pal, Jim Ewing, had to go in to the weir and drag him out to save him.

We had a lovely little black cat called Bovril who we thought of as an 'honorary dog'. Unfortunately, poor old Bovers got run down by a car and killed. My wife was quite heartbroken over poor old Bov – and so was I, to be fair. He was a lovely cat. The pub in the village, in Stoke Golding, was selling kittens for £15 and they had a black one, a female, which I purchased, thinking it would be a good idea. It turned out to be the most horrible cat in the world – spawned by the devil. It absolutely hated me. I don't know why, because I was never bad to it, but I think it pretty much hated everybody. I was in bed one day and I woke up to find the cat had shat on my bed and pissed on it while I'd been sleeping. I knew the cat had just done it for spite – it was like that. I thought, "That's it, the cat goes, or I take it and drown it in the canal." In the end, one of Sophie's nutty colleagues took it in, but I don't think she had much luck with it either. Anyway, good riddance to bad rubbish, as far as I'm concerned.

We bought a house in Sheridan Street, just off the Aylestone Road. It was a little terraced two-bedroomed house, with a little back yard like a "Coronation Street" house. It needed a great deal of work doing to it, especially since the people who lived in it before us had two kids and obviously the kids had run riot with crayon. It was pretty run down really, but we got that house for a pretty cheap price. We spent some money doing it up, with new windows. I, of course, rewired it and we put in electric central heating and storage heaters, mainly because I could do it, which would be so much cheaper that having gas put in. We made a nice house out of that and of course Samson was with us.

Sophie went to Bath with her pal Liz for the day in summer 1996. Samson, at the time, was about two years old. Anyway, I was on my own and bored and started to read the small ads in the local paper, which is something I never really do.

Talking about small ads, my pal Jim used to love reading small ads and the death notices. When Jim was reading these notices he announced, "I see we've got three "peacefullys" today, one "suddenly" and four "quietlys". He would do this every time he read the death column in the local paper.

Anyway, I digress. I found an advert advertising a German Shepherd puppy for re-homing so I had to buy it. I phoned the owner up and went to see him about the dog. I took Sam with me so that the owner would see that I had a dog and that Sam was well looked after. Sadly, the owner couldn't have given a toss about where his dog was going. The owner invited me and Sam into his house and brought the dog in from the back of the house. Following this dog was the biggest German Shepherd dog I have ever seen! Samson shit himself (not literally!) when he saw this great big dog coming towards him! Sam ended up on my lap on this guy's sofa, petrified of this giant dog!

Sasha was the dog that the guy wanted to re-home. She was a frail thing, awfully skinny and she looked as though she hadn't been particularly well looked after. Sasha was six months old. I asked the guy what food Sasha ate and also if she was house trained. The owner said, "Oh yes". I was pleased about that so I paid the guy his money and left with a new dog. I took the dog home.

When Sophie came back from her day trip to Bath she said, "What the fuck is this?"

I said, "This is Sasha."

Sophie wasn't very happy about the new acquisition but she kind of got round to the idea, until Sasha chewed five of her best shoes – one shoe each from five different pairs! Five pairs of shoes ruined including her knee length boots! It took Sasha a long time to ingratiate herself back into Sophie's favour. On top of this, Sasha wasn't house trained at all, but to be fair to her, she learned very quickly. It was however, a sore point between Sophie and me for a while but not as sore as the point about the shoes. As my condition improved I was back out walking the dogs.

In September 1998, Sasha and Samson were married! They got it together and three months later, Sasha had a litter of eleven pups although one was stillborn. Five pups were delivered at home and Sasha was exhausted. A rush to the vet saw Sasha have a caesarean section to deliver the remaining six puppies, followed by a hysterectomy. Two days later, she was jumping on and off the couch!

Ten puppies, two adult dogs and two humans in a two bedroomed terraced house – pandemonium, but great!

Sasha produced no milk, therefore the puppies had to be fed by Sophie and me using the fingers of a rubber glove. Preparing their food and clearing up took four hours, by which time the whole process started all over again! Friends came to take on a shift to allow us to go to bed.

Initially, the dogs all lived in a pen in the house, but when the puppies were four weeks old they all got out of the pen and climbed the stairs, leaving a trail of destruction, including the killing of our prize rubber plant.

We successfully looked after the pups until they were eight weeks old. At this point we sold eight of them and kept two, Chester, and Scooter – the runt of the litter. Our friends, Jim and Theresa, took Corrie. Sophie's mum, Lesley, took Buster, two couples took one pup each and my university lecturer took another. Bonnie went to a Game-keeper on an estate in the Scottish Borders and two more went to another person.

This is another holiday story, going back years ago when we had the four Shepherd dogs: Samson, Sasha, Jester and Scooter. We had rented a holiday cottage down in Devon. One of Sophie's colleagues owned it and she was quite happy for us to take the dogs down, which was really nice of her. I travelled down on the bike, while

Sophie went down in the trusty Volvo, and we arrived in North Devon at this lovely little cottage. It was nice until we lost the keys, of course, and were locked out. I hitched over the back garden and fortunately, we had left a window open. I climbed in and took the snib off the door, but we had to phone up Sophie's colleague and get her to send a spare set of keys down so we could lock up.

When Samson got to about 10 years old, he started to show signs of aggression, which was something the old boy had never done. We lived in Avebury Avenue at the time and I had Samson at the park. I had been throwing the ball for him and I asked him to leave the ball and he wouldn't – which was, again, unusual. I bent down to take the ball from his mouth and he launched himself at me and bit me on the head. He kept biting me, so I rolled myself into a ball and he bit me on the shoulder and arm. Then he stopped and carried on as though nothing had happened and everything was normal! I took him to the vet and explained the situation and it turned out that Samson had a benign tumour pressing on his brain. The vet said there was nothing he could do about the tumour, that it would get worse but would not cause the dog any pain. The situation did get worse and Samson bit Sophie. So, while the dog was not in pain, we were – and it was certainly affecting Samson's rationale, which was a concern. We kept Samson for another three years, managing by ignoring his odd behaviour and keeping him away from people. In the end, however, we had to have Samson put to sleep. I had lost my old dog by then – he was completely 'doo-lally': a bit like dog dementia. He didn't recognise people he once knew, developed a nasty temper and lost control of his faculties. It was very sad.

Chapter 8

My mum had died in the September '92 so Christmas '92 wasn't really a good time as it was my first Christmas without her. Sophie's mum had invited me round for Christmas dinner, but I wanted to be on my own and be a miserable git, so I said I'd go round after they'd eaten and see them in the evening. Sophie's mum had put on a bit of a spread and had a nice cheese board and I was invited to help myself so I duly did. I helped myself to the ends of a few bits of cheese, thinking that was probably the place to start, but seemingly Steve was pissed off because the ends of the cheese – the pointy bits if you like, are the best bits, and here I was! This man had come in and taken the best bits of his cheese! He was pretty cheesed off! A strange thing!

I remember going up to York with Sophie on the train to see my sister Joyce who we'd arranged to meet. We had a good day. We went to the York railway museum. It's a good day out for anybody, even if you're not that particularly interested in trains – just a fabulous place to go and see the development of trains from all over the world. Anyway, I digress! So we had a good day in York and we got the train back home, which broke down in Derby. This was about midnight. They eventually found us a taxi that would take us all the way to Leicester. It was a black cab with five people in it who lived in various different parts of Northamptonshire and of course, because we lived the furthest away, we were the last to be dropped off. It took us about three hours to get home, arriving home at 3am! So that was a bit of a "bummer" on a good day, but there you are!

So Sophie had been in New Zealand with her brothers, gran, mum and stepdad for about six years from the age of twelve till about eighteen. She hadn't seen her dad during this time so she was re-united with her dad, David, when she came back to England. We found out that David had cancer of the colon and basically didn't have a lot of time left, so we used to go down to see him every fortnight, or more, if we could get the time off work. We also visited her granddad, Herbert.

I liked David and I wish I could have got to know him a bit better. He was a really, really, clever bloke. One of those chaps who can fix anything. You know, he just had the knack for fixing stuff. I'd like to have got to know him a bit better for himself and also because I could have picked his brains. He was a clever bloke and I could have learned a lot from him. Sophie's mum, Lesley, is clever as well. So with a combination of both mum and dad, I can see where Sophie and her brothers got their brains from.

It was sad when David died. We used to go down and see him and just used to potter about really, and when he was admitted into the hospice that was sad. I remember when he died I felt really bad for Sophie because I'd lost my dad when I'd just turned seventeen, so I knew the pain she was feeling and especially as she'd just recently been reunited with him. You know, after six years to get only six months with him seemed like a kick in the teeth, really.

Looking back, being kicked in the teeth is all Sophie and I have known for a long time, so maybe it was just a taster of things to come. Sophie and I had to cremate her dad and dispose of the contents of his house, which we did at a car boot sale, sadly. Horrible places, people scrabbling over your stuff. Sophie and I went to Cromer to scatter David's ashes in the sea, and that was sad. Not helped by me being in a bad mood, if I remember – which was just wrong, of course. Samson came with us and David being a Merchant seaman, we cast his ashes into the sea. It is a sad thing to do. Is it better to keep the ashes? We thought it would be nicer for David to be at sea. I don't know. Everybody's got their own ideas about that.

Not long after, her granddad Herbert died, so we had all that to sort out as well. The sad thing about Herbert was that he was one of about ten kids who was born just after the turn of the nineteenth century, and when his mum died, his dad couldn't cope. So Herbert and the rest of the kids were put up for adoption and scattered to the four corners of the world. They all lost touch with one another, so there are people out there who are related to Sophie but don't know her or her brothers, nor that Herbert has died, and that seems so sad.

I remember we used to go down and stay at her Grandpa's house and Samson the dog pissed on the bloody bed. Aw, typical! So, not surprisingly, we got a bollocking from Herbert. I wanted to kick the dog's arse. I don't know why Samson did that. He was normally pretty good although he did have three strange spells in his life; one at the end of his life when he got dog dementia, one when he dug up Lesley's mums carpet between the hall and the kitchen – and then he pissed on the bed at the same time. He was obviously trying to tell us something!

So, all in all, with the passing of Sophie's dad and granddad, it was sad time.

I started a new job with Vodafone. It was a year's contract I signed, on the basis that I wouldn't be away from home too often and I'd be home most nights. What a lot of shit! They lied. I was away more often than not, living in crap digs. I remember that after six months, it was part of the contract that they gave you sick pay if you went 'on the sick'. By then, I was knackered anyway, so I went to the doctor and got signed off work with stress and got paid from them for six months. I think it served the bastards right, because they had deceived me and if they had told me the truth, I wouldn't have taken the job. So, that got them back!

Vodafone employed a bunch of numpties to maintain their mobile phone connections – the grey boxes at the side of motorways. We used to do them. As an electrician I thought it was my job to do the electrical work while my assistant did the unpacking but Vodafone didn't see it that way – and nor did my assistant. I was new to the company, so the assistant was giving me all the shitty jobs. One day he had put all his back-up batteries on the rack: great big batteries. He actually managed to short out the battery power on the frame of the cabinet. This was all very well, but the metal cabinet – the batteries on the frame and the little box frame were made of aluminium. The door was closed and he basically spot-welded everything shut! The door was welded to the door frame. It took a hell of an age to break these welds – even against the door. I complained to the powers that be about letting people like that loose on electrics, but it made absolutely no difference. That was the power of the spot-welding assistant.

I remember one night after Sophie and I had been out, when poor old Sophie had had one drink too many. She had acquired a taste for Guinness, for some reason. Horrible stuff! We were going back to my house, and I managed to get her home. She was pretty pissed, it has to be said, and she said she was feeling really, really ill. In fact, she was going to be sick. The only thing I could grab, in time for her to be sick in, was my 'piece' box: my sandwich box, which she pretty much chucked the entire contents of her stomach into and filled up. My job was to hold her hair out of this pizza topping. Eugh! I remember that!

Poor girl, she wasn't used to alcohol. I don't know if her mum and stepdad Steve were very religious, but they'd joined the Mormon Church – don't ask me why, and Sophie and her brothers all got dragged along too, although they didn't want to go. I remember it was a concern of Sophie's father, David, that the kids were getting brainwashed. I think it was pretty obvious that all three of his kids were way too sharp to get sucked into that, though. When Sophie had moved in with me, either Sophie's mum or Steve had given the Mormons my address, and they bloody pestered her for weeks. In the end, I went to the door to tell them that Sophie was an adult, who could make up her own mind, and if she wanted to go back to the Mormons, she was free to do so. But until then, they were to stop coming to the house – which they duly did, to be fair. They never came back.

One of the times when we were down at Sophie's dad's before he died, we had a terrible night of rain and it'd been rumbling with thunder. I think we went down to the beach and sat in the old van when sheet lightning started up. I've never seen sheet lightning and I was quite fascinated by it. Rather than the stuff that goes from heaven to earth it just kind of stays in the heavens and lights up half the sky: it was marvellous! I was dead impressed, anyway.

Another time we were down there we were walking along the beach and I fell into what appeared to be quicksand. In fact, a ship had dumped a whole load of engine oil into the sea, which had washed up onto the shore, and had then been covered in sand. I sunk into it about half way up my ankles, which was all very well, but my boots, socks, trousers, and feet were covered in this thick gunky engine oil. That might have been ok but I was going out that night for a pub meal with Sophie and David, so I ended up wearing tracksuit bottoms and a pair of trainers. I don't think David was impressed, but I really couldn't help it.

Anyway, we'll go onto speak about the characters in the Three Horseshoes pub that Sophie worked in. There were a couple of people that stood out, and I think they must have been twins, a young man and a young woman. They had the strangest faces. They looked like gawping goldfish. I called them Captain Fishy and his sister, Fishy

Fingers. I don't know why, but we gave everybody a name. That was just one of the things we did.

Two blokes walked into the bar where Sophie worked and ordered a couple of pints of bitter. One chap took himself off to the loo and brought out a handful of change and said, "Can you just take the money out of there?"

To which my wife-to-be replied, "Why can't you do it yourself? Are you blind or something?"

The guy replied, "Actually, yes I am."

That was a bit of an embarrassment for her!

It was nearly Christmas when I'd just met Sophie and of course I was mad about her, as you know. So we went down to the Coach and Horses which was run by a Glaswegian who we'll call Frank, although that wasn't his name. I went down with Davie and Hughie for a few beers after Christmas and we walked in. The bar wasn't stowed out but it wasn't quiet either, so we ordered a beer and the barman, Frank, said to me, "Where's your girlfriend tonight?"

"Oh, she's working down at the Three Horseshoes," I said.

To which he replied, "Oh, I didn't know they had strippers working there!"

So Frank got dragged across the bar and would've been dragged all the way over if it hadn't been for the bottle opener attached to the bar catching on his belt. So basically, he was saved by the belt, but I still managed to get a few swings in before Davie and Hughie finally pulled me off him. Frank was actually very apologetic, and so he should have been, because he could've got a really good hiding. I was on a high dose of steroids and had a very quick temper.

I knew this couple called Terry and June. They used to run the Coach and Horses before Tam aka Frank took over. I think Davie Smith ended up knocking off Terry's missus. Then they left. Anyway, they had a little dog about the size of a Staffy terrier. It had amazingly large testicles, like grapefruits. I don't know if there was anything wrong with this dog but it was almost like he had big bits missing out of his legs to accommodate them. It always used to make me laugh, this dog with these unfeasibly large testicles who could barely walk properly because of them.

Before I met Sophie and even when I was going out with her and wasn't working, I used to go round all the different shops for my groceries, plus the butcher, the baker and candlestick maker, and then cart it all home. I used to live quite well, actually, foodwise and didn't eat a lot of rubbish. I think my drinking kind of slowed up, too, when I was with Sophie, which was no bad thing, really.

Sophie always wanted to go to the fair. I would never go willingly, because I used to take her around the fair during the daylight and point out all the dodgy electrics that these people could get away with from their big generators. So there was no danger we'd be going to the fair if I had anything to do with it. Probably get killed by electrocution.

Before Sophie moved in we got rid of Mr Odd because he was just plain, fucking weird. Yeah, we just told him we were getting rid of all the lodgers and that I was having the house back to myself which was clearly not the case –

but anyway, he went. We got Dave Smith's pal, Hughie, who was also a Scottish ex-paratrooper, to move in. Funnily enough, he liked a drink as well, so we all got on famously.

Sophie moved in with me after six months, in May '93. We got on like a house on fire and she was due to start her medical training at Leicester University in the October. I must admit I was in a right state about this, because I thought once she went up there and saw younger fitter men, I'd be kicked into touch. Obviously I'd told her about my illness by this time.

When I was first diagnosed with low grade lymphoma I was given a "mean" time of 13 years to live, but it was often changed depending on the next thing that happened to go wrong for me medically, with each new time being shorter than the one before. So around that time, I'd been told I had around ten years to live and I was really concerned that Sophie was going to be up and off when she went to university. She didn't, fortunately, but I wasn't to know that, and all I could do was basically hope it wouldn't come to that.

I remember moving her into the halls of residence using my trusty white escort diesel van. Her room was a tiny little place, and I remember it had just one 5 amp socket so I had to make an extension lead up for all her various computers and hairdryer, curling tongs, hair straighteners and goodness knows what else that Sophie used to keep herself young and beautiful! It was a filthy place, actually. The people in her halls were lazy, dirty bastards. They wouldn't clean or do any washing up and when their plates were dirty they would help themselves to other people's crockery. It was just a shit hole. But hey ho, she got over it and completed her first year with the usual aplomb. I used to go up to Leicester and stay for a couple of days in the week and then Sophie would come back to my house if she could.

My fears about being dumped came to nothing – and I'm glad about that, obviously. I should also add that when I was working for Vodafone I had to go down and do an induction course at Newbury and that's where I bought her a pair of walking boots, a waterproof jacket and a little gold locket because she was saving the money she was earning. Sophie had two jobs, one in a lab in the afternoon and one in a pub at night where she was a short order cook, making hamburgers and so on, and she used to work the bar at the weekends. She was saving up all her money for university and because of this, the arse was falling out of her jeans, metaphorically speaking, her boots and jacket were well worn and when we used to go for these walks, she wasn't really very well equipped. So I bought her these things, along with a locket – heart shaped, of course. I think Steve was pissed off about me spending money on his stepdaughter but she was well worth it and great company.

In March '94 we got engaged, and I remember we went to a little jeweller's in a street just off Northampton town centre and there was a second hand diamond solitaire ring that she liked. I think it was the princely sum of £125 actually, which was the ring that Sophie wanted. She might have wanted a bigger diamond, and probably did, but times were hard and as I say, interest rates were phenomenal, so yeah, we got engaged. In August '94, we got married.

Sophie and I got married on a Friday. My stag do was held on the Wednesday, two days prior to the wedding. All the lads who were coming up from England were there: Shaun, Trevor, Rennie, and Jim. I'd asked Jim to get in touch with a few other guys from Perth, so there were fifteen of us in total. We decided to have a kitty, so everyone stuck in a tenner to begin with, as that would be enough to get us started. We gave the money to big Shaun who was a power lifter. He looked pretty impressive physically and we thought that no one would bother him. I also bargained on him staying sober because his body was a temple to him, but because he never normally drank, after two or three pints of Guinness he was beginning to show a bit of wear and tear. However, he saw it to the end of the night and he was good. We visited several pubs around the town and we were all pretty drunk, because we had to top up the kitty with another tenner. Also, we visited pubs we wouldn't normally go to, just to try somewhere different.

At about 11.30, we all went roaring drunk up to the York House Hotel because they had a disco there on a Wednesday. It was mainly filled by student nurses, and in days gone by, it was always a favourite haunt of mine. They had kind hearts! Fortunately, my pal Jim knew the doorman through biking, and was quite friendly with him. Trevor was bouncing off walls, falling down and generally being drunk. The doorman said to Jim, "I can't let your mate in, in that state."

I knew the doorman too, and said, "Look, Steve, our mate may look really pissed but he's not that bad. He's recently lost his leg in an accident and he's not quite used to his prosthetic limb. So maybe you could cut him a bit of slack."

The doorman said, "Ok, but you guys must look after him – he's bouncing off the walls like a pin-ball!"

We assured Steve the doorman that we would do that. Once we got inside, everyone went to different parts of the hotel. Some of the lads went upstairs to the balcony, looking down onto the dance floor, others spread around the various bar and Jim and I were in the downstairs bar. I think it was called The Log Cabin – tasteful, eh?

So, me and Jim are having a drink when the doorman Steve comes in and says, "You're going to have to come and sort your mate out. He's causing bother – he's walking about with his nob out. He's flashing all over the building. The girls are shrieking."

And so we had to go and sort him, and sure enough, Trevor is trying to negotiate his way down the stairs with his willy hanging out, and everyone is trampling over each other, trying to get away from him. We got Trevor downstairs, told him to put his willy away, then put him on a sofa parked under the staircase, where he promptly fell asleep.

At this point I was working as a doorman at various clubs including Northampton and Cambridge. It was at this time that the steroids were making me aggressive and a lot of people did remark on the size of me. I used to train with a couple of guys at Karate, Chris and Van, and they used to advise people not to annoy me, as I used to knock them about at the karate training. The reason I put on so much weight was because my appetite had increased due to taking steroids, but it was mainly because of the training I did with Shaun, the power lifter. I was just always riled and that was the effect of the steroids.

We went up to Perth the following year and climbed Kinnoull Hill. It's about 500 feet. It's not too strenuous, with a nice winding path round, although I couldn't do it now, of course. Again, me, Samson and Sophie all trooped up to the top where there was about a foot of snow. Sophie and I built a giant snowman and thoroughly enjoyed ourselves. I was just like a big kid around Sophie. She used to make me so happy, and continued to do so.

Once I got over the shock and rage, and accepted my illness, I was able to channel that anger into doing more training. I was pushing myself harder and harder in the gym, drinking less alcohol and eating very healthily. But even in my more positive moments, I could still slip back into being angry. When I couldn't get rid of my frustrations through training, I took it out on Sophie. I'm not proud of that, but it's the way it happened, and because she was there, she was first in the firing line. Luckily, my wife is smart and she knew the difference between my normal behaviour and which aspects of my behaviour were linked to the effects the drugs were having on me.

I remember a specific incident while I was on steroids, when I used to get quite angry. The effect of the steroids seemed to be like an on/off switch. One minute I was calm, and the next minute someone would say something to me and I'd get very angry. However, it was just a trigger rather than the real cause of my anger: my fury was bitterness and frustration at my illness, deep down. I wouldn't back down from people in pubs; I was always looking for a fight to get the anger out of me.

Being ill is a great leveller and when you have to rely on people to help you, you are humbled. I suppose the illness has made me a more sympathetic person. During the past twenty years, I met and married Sophie and she has been a huge support to me whilst still managing to become a successful doctor. I appreciate my wife more and I've learned to value Sophie greatly throughout our marriage. But when you're not well, you always take it out on the ones who are closest to you.

I've never, ever, hit my wife but I remember one time that I think I was going to, which is a horrible thing to say, but I was angry, I was ill and I just went for her. It was all too much. Too much for anyone to take, and I just blew! I was coming across the room towards Sophie, furious, and she obviously thought I was going to hit her. What else do you do when a furious guy pumped up on steroids with nothing to lose comes flying for you? She grabbed the jug of an antique basin and jug set, and belted me round the head with it as hard as she could! Of course, I collapsed unconscious, blood spurting out of my head wound.

I'd have told you I never knew what hit me, but unfortunately, I did.

When I was coming round she said, crossly, "Hold the

towel on your head!" and meekly, I did as I was told.

She went and got a normal needle and thread to stitch me up.

"Ow! Bloody hell! Shouldn't I be anaesthetised?" I muttered.

"I'll happily anaesthetise you in a minute," she said through gritted teeth, squinting to thread the cotton into the eye of the needle. "Just pass me the matching basin, and I'll knock you out again."

"No, but seriously… should you take me to casualty?" I asked innocently. "For something to kill the pain?"

"I'm not wasting my time off work sitting in A&E! I spend thirty hours a day at hospital as it is!" she cried, pressing two sides of my split scalp together with two pinched fingers. "I haven't got any stuff to kill the pain, so just let it be a lesson to you." She jabbed the needle into my head.

This is just how cruel my wife is. I am joking, by the way – just in case she does come at me with the basin this time. It's heavier.

"You're not doing blanket stitch are you?" I winced, imagining her getting further revenge on my outburst by making me wear great big Frankenstein's monster needlework across my face.

"Cross-stitch," she said, crossly.

Sophie didn't take the attack I made on her, personally. She did what she had to do in the circumstances – she sparked me out, then she stitched me up! It was a turning point. I had all this anger pent up inside me. Unfortunately, I was so ill and worn out, I wasn't able to train at this point, so had no physical outlet for my pent-up fury. Although walking the dogs is good exercise, it wasn't the same as completely exhausting myself at the gym. I learned a lesson from that, not because of the pain, but because I realised that my wife was good to me and if I kept up that sort of nonsense she would leave – and frankly, I wouldn't blame her. There have been a lot of steep learning curves!

My trusted dog Max

Scooter

Sasha & Jester　　　　　*Joyce & Noreen at my wedding*

Duncan

The Yellow Peril

Glenn Finnan Viaduct

My Trike

Bathtime

My business, Will Electrical

Trevor, my one-legged friend

My last walk

Me, Summer 2013

Chapter 9

Although I was married at the time, I was up in Scotland on my own. I'd been in town and bought a couple of Murray's pies for my dinner. Murray's pies, looking back, were probably a heart attack on a plate anyway, full of minced mutton, plus any bits of sawdust they could shovel in. So perhaps it's just as well, what happened. Anyway, I got terrible food poisoning from these pies, with vomiting and diarrhoea. I was staying at Jim's mum and dad's at the time, and fortunately, their sink is adjacent to the toilet, so while I was spray painting the toilet pan in shit I was also spray painting the sink in vomit. It was so bad that once I'd cleared my innards out, I took to my bed with a jug of water and was never seen again for the next 24 hours! Of course, Mrs Ewing was frantically worried, but was too scared to come into the room in case I was dead. She had to get her son to come in and check, because poor old Margaret and John Ewing didn't want to find a corpse in their spare room bed.

Another episode in my life - I've never eaten Murray's pies since!

I know I sold the white van and Sophie gave me her old car when she got her dad's new Escort after he had died. I got Sophie's old Escort – a sky blue one it was, 1300cc. It was bloody noisy, I remember that. You couldn't hear yourself think. It was like going to a rock concert, you know, having your ears messed with, but it did the job.

To get it to start when it wouldn't because of the damp, Sophie used to clean the plugs and points in that old thing, and took the distributor off and all that malarkey. She was quite intrepid really. Eventually, I sold the Escort and I think we traded in her dad's Escort, which was very heavy on the steering, for the Volvo, which we were ever so chuffed about. We loved that car. Big and white and we felt really quite posh in it.

The Volvo was a great car, which we bought just before my transplant. Sophie took the Volvo to a car wash one day, the type that pulls you through as the big brushes come down. Unfortunately, Sophie hadn't lined the car up properly and it was only on one track. So as she was going through the wash, the side of the car was getting scraped along all the equipment and she didn't know what to do to stop the car wash process. Net result, our lovely Volvo was scraped from the front to the back with dents in the doors. It was just a mess! Fortunately, we took it to a chap, a little one-man-band panel beater and he made a beautiful job of repairing it for a very reasonable price. So it wasn't so bad in the end!

The old Volvo estate was a 240 Torslanda. We loved that car! It was like sitting in a tank: you didn't feel in the least bit vulnerable. We thought it was great and since I'd bought a van for my work, towards the end of the car's life I gave it to Trev, who was needing a car and had been working for me for a couple of weeks. It lasted all of a week with Trevor, who managed to ram it into the side of a brand new van! It didn't do a great deal of damage to the Volvo but I think the new van was pretty much totalled!

The Volvo had a bent wing and cracked head lamp and the bumper was shot, but apart from that, it still drove ok. Looking back, it might have been worth fixing, but Trevor got rid of it. We went everywhere in this old Volvo. It was the height of luxury as far as we were concerned. It was like driving a tank and you could get all sorts of stuff in it.

I've had lots of jobs. After my transplant, I didn't feel well enough to work but I didn't want to be doing nothing. So when I came out after my transplant I had applied to go to Sheffield Hallam University, as they had an annexe in Leicester. I didn't have any "O" Levels because although I sat them, I wasn't motivated to do any work for them as I didn't care whether I passed them or not. They told me that because I had no "O" Levels I would need to do an Access Course. I made enquiries about the Sports Science Course at Hallam, as I thought I might like to become a coach, and people had told me they thought I was a good Karate coach. So, I got myself onto this Access Course in the September but I had to give that up in November because of the liver and kidney failure. Once I got over the liver and kidney failure I asked if I could get back on the Access Course the following September and the university agreed. I completed the course and then I applied to do an HND at Sheffield Hallam, which I did.

I loved the course and enjoyed being at University three days a week and studying at home. From having my transplant in 1995, it took four years to complete my HND. Then I decided I would do my Degree in Sports Science. I got accepted into the third year of the Course at Bedford University, which was quite far away from home.

Coventry said they'd accept me but only into the second year, but I didn't want to do two more years of study. However, it became clear very quickly that travelling to Bedford on a daily basis was not sustainable. I wrote to the tutor and apologised profusely for taking up a place that someone else could have had. However, I didn't know I couldn't sustain it until I tried! That was my "work", as it were, for the first four years after my transplant.

After this, I put my HND to good use and got a job as a gym instructor with Living Well – which I called 'Living Hell'! The gym instructors who were there had all done YMCA courses and their knowledge was nil! It was also very cliquey and because I was over-qualified for the gym, the instructors never really took to me. I didn't like their attitude. We got paid extra money for doing extra classes, but I was never given a lot of opportunity to do them. The opportunities were given to their mates. When I left the company, I said I didn't feel I was being recognised and used to my full potential. When I was working in the gym, I knew I needed to be as fit or fitter than my clients, so I pushed myself to the point that I was very fit again. I didn't mention to anyone what I'd been through.

I sat my HGV licence before my transplant. It had been a boyhood ambition to hold this licence and learn to drive a truck. It always amazed me how these men put that huge truck into such small openings, so I always wanted to do that. Prior to transplant, when the medics told me the prognosis wasn't good, I thought I should realise my boyhood ambition and sit and pass the test. So, when I left the gym, and although I'd never used my HGV licence, I signed on with a couple of Driving Agencies and started driving a truck. I enjoyed the journeys and staying away overnight, and because my day was filled and effectively, I was my own boss. It was up to me to plan my journey to make those deliveries on time. I enjoy my own company, and I could listen to the radio and read books.

I drove only in Britain, except on one occasion when I agreed to do a private job for a friend. I drove a HGV to and from France when I helped a friend remove his elderly mother's belongings from her home in France back to Britain, after 30 years. The mother spoke fluent French, knew all her neighbours and seemed very settled. I don't know why she agreed to come back to Britain! It seemed to me that she could easily have lived many more years in France!

I was never away for more than a couple of nights at a time. There was no real camaraderie in the agencies. I only had two company trucking jobs. One was with a local company called Speedy Dispatch, who were a great bunch of blokes to work with. The boss was great and took us out for a curry every Friday night. He only had 5 or 6 drivers. He worked us hard but he wouldn't ask us to do anything he wasn't prepared to do himself. I respected him.

One Friday night we had all gone down to the Bees Knees pub prior to going for a curry. There was me, Dave the boss, Wayne, the Transport Manager, plus Gordon, Chris and another bloke, Jim, who was only about twenty-five years old and the youngest of us all. He was as thick as a brick, really. He knew this girl who was under sixteen years old, and he used to take this young girl away in the truck with him. It didn't sit easy with me, but obviously her mother didn't give a fuck because the guy was sleeping at the mother's house with the girl anyway.

Normally when we were in the pub the young girl would join us but on this particular night she didn't appear and Dave asked Jim, "Where is your girlfriend tonight?"

Jim replied, "She's studying for her exams."

I asked "Which exams are these? The 11-plus?"

Dave and the rest of the company burst out laughing but the joke was wasted on Jim!

During the time that my arthritis began to play up and I was waiting to get my hips replaced, we used to do a lot of concrete block deliveries. The concrete factory expected us truck drivers to load these blocks onto the back of the truck ourselves. It got to the stage when I just couldn't do it. The blocks were too heavy for me to manoeuvre. My boss got in touch with them and said, "One of my drivers can't do this, so can you help him?" He always made sure I got a hand, or got jobs that were lighter and I could manage.

I didn't stay forever because he was having difficulties with his Mrs who was basically running the company down and taking money out of it. Dave, the boss, knew what his wife was up to. He then joined her and helped her to finish running the business into the ground!

While we were living in the Brook House in Stokegolding, I left Speedy's but continued with the Agencies and applied for a job with Wincanton Haulage. I'd gone back to the agencies because I didn't really think that anybody would employ me, with my medical history. Working for the agencies meant that I could get work, just days here and there. Money was a bit tight, so we came to the decision that it would be better if I got a permanent job. Hence the application to Wincanton. They were advertising for drivers on the night shift, so I wrote off, explaining to them all that had happened to me. On paper it looked like I was a wreck, but in actual fact I was more than capable of driving a truck. I explained that I'd had a transplant but that I was able to function normally, hold down a job and earn a living. They had me for an interview.

I was asked all the usual questions: "What do you think you can bring to Wincanton?" "

"An HGV Class 1 licence. I can bring that," I said

The interviewers found this quite amusing and said, "OK, anything else?"

I said, "Well, it's a job driving a truck. What else would you want me to bring? I've got a licence, I'm here and I'm willing to do the work."

The interview panel conferred and then asked, "Why Wincanton specifically?"

I replied, "There was no 'specifically' Wincanton. I'm actually quite willing to work full-time for anybody – the reason being that my wife wants a new kitchen and I need to get into full-time employment to pay for it."

The interviewers thought I was joking and said they liked my sense of humour. They thought they'd enjoy working with me.

I said, "But I'm not trying to be funny."

This brought out more laughs from the interviewers – I think they thought I was a comedian! It went downhill from there.

That job went well for a while and then, as winter came, I would get chest infections and I had to take time off. Because I had taken time off I was interviewed for what they call 'the back to work interview.' I think it's more of an 'I've got my eye on you.' They asked me why, given that the average Wincanton employee takes 3.5 days off a year, I'd had 7 days absence from work in half that time. I explained that I'd had cancer and my immune system was shot. They hadn't realised this and thought I was going to be as fit as the next man!

I had to go and see their Occupational Health nurse who didn't know what GVH was and was completely out of her depth. She advised the boss that I shouldn't be driving a truck until I had confirmation from the DVLA. I had already informed the DVLA of my situation and confirmed that I was allowed to drive. However, Wincanton wanted to check with the DVLA for themselves. They told me that in the meantime I would be on yard duties which involved standing on my feet for 8 hours, checking things out. When you've got bad hips, that's not an easy job to do.

I said, "I have a contract to say that I am employed to drive a truck. If I'm not driving a truck, then I'll get signed off by the doctor!"

So the boss asked if I'd be prepared to be the yard shunter and I said yes, that would be fine. To be a yard shunter, you need to do a test even although you have a

HGV licence, as the job is slightly different. The chap who was doing the shunting was the trainer and he said, "Well, if he's not driving a truck, he's not drivin' a shunt vehicle."

I began to get really angry with them all, because they couldn't seem to work anything out. It never really got sorted. I found that the yard staff and the warehouse staff never spoke to the truck driving staff and it was all really cliquey and horrible. I was put back onto truck driving in the end and went in one night to start at 6 o' clock in the evening but my load wasn't ready. However, the 7pm load was ready but the driver wasn't in till 7. So, I said, "Give me the 7 o' clock load and I'll go, and by the time the 6 o'clock load is ready the 7pm chap can drive that."

I was told that couldn't happen because it mucked up the system and the guy wasn't going to do that. I persisted with this and we began to argue about the situation. In the end I said to the guy, "Look, here's your key, shove it up your arse!"

I don't like working with idiots – it would have been a benefit to them to have me out on the road making a delivery. I used to drive regularly but now I get bored with driving long distances. I just get so fed-up, sitting in a car for miles and miles.

After this, I became self-employed in my old trade, as an electrician. I wrote to several kitchen fitting companies and explained that I'd just started up and asked if there was any work I could do for them. I did this, despite being ill, for 2.5 years. By this point, I had burned myself out and had to give up work but I think I'd given it my best shot up until then. So that was that!

I could've just sat in my bed and been ill, but I think if I'd done that I would've been dead. I had a friend who had the same illness as me, diagnosed years after me and he is now dead. His attitude was, "I am ill!" He never went to work after his diagnosis and was served on, hand and foot, by his wife. He lasted maybe 8 years. He got a transplant but carried on drinking heavily, smoking heavily and ended up with lung cancer. His lymphoma never quite went away and I think some sort of metastases occurred. I think your attitude and the way you think has a lot to do with your survival. If you think you're finished, then you're half way there already.

Around September/October time in 1994, I started to suffer from liver failure. This was in part due to me having problems with the anti-rejection drugs I was on. The drugs caused me to have a high biliruben count. I'm led to believe that a healthy person's liver should have a reading of around 20. My biliruben count peaked at 1050. My general condition began to deteriorate and whatever the medics tried, didn't work. I just kept getting worse and worse.

It got to the point one day when I was visiting the hospital as an out-patient with my sister Joyce, I was told by a nurse that I only had three weeks to live and that I would need to decide where I wanted to die.

Joyce: Due to your liver problems your movements were slow and very sluggish. But you had a huge desire to survive and to be in control of whatever you could.

Norman: A control freak.

Joyce: Hardly. You had a wart on your thumb that was annoying you. You set the same goal for yourself each day in an effort to get rid of the wart. Slowly you got yourself out of bed, came downstairs, sat down and painted the wart with solution. By the time you had carried out this process, you were exhausted but you "dug deep" and used what strength you had to return upstairs to your bed. After a few weeks, your wart cleared up!

Norman: I beat the bastard.

Joyce: Goal accomplished – so small but so significant. During this time your skin was the colour of English mustard. I accompanied you to a hospital appointment at Leicester Royal. After it, a nurse asked to speak to us privately.

Norman: She was a cow.

Joyce: She was professional in her manner, but not very warm, as she explained to you how ill you were. Although I don't remember what she said word for word, the gist of it was that you didn't look as though you were likely to survive, and if you wanted to die in hospital you really needed to let the hospital know.

Norman: Book-a-bed-ahead!

Joyce: I was horrified at the situation but you turned to me
            and said, "Tell her I'm not dying," and with that you
            stood up and we left the room.

I moved up to Leicester to see about a transplant.
Leicester Royal was the nearest hospital to me that could
do transplants, I suppose. I basically pitched up there to
hear what they had to say. There was a diagnosis, there
was treatment, there was a plateau that they held it to,
and then you became ill again – and that's when the bone
marrow transplant was considered. After 5 years of being
on chemotherapy in tablet form, on and off, on and off, my
body stopped responding, basically. By now I had several
cancerous growths over my head and that was when I
was coming to the end of my five years and it kicked off.
At that point, I probably had about six months to live. I
never knew that, Joyce told me recently. I was referred to
Leicester and saw Dr Hutchison, who's since retired. He
said that I would have to have a bone marrow transplant
or that would be it. That was the choice – no choice. If we
didn't attempt the bone marrow transplant, then I would
be dead shortly. He told me the facts and I agreed to go
with his plan.

After a couple of days post-transplant, I could drag
myself to the en suite bathroom to shower. It was vital to
avoid infection. The hospital had this anti-bacterial soap
called *Aquasept* which was an all-over disinfectant soap.
It killed everything in its path. If you had a scab or a skin
infection, within one wash all the bacteria were completely
destroyed and the wound was healing up! One of our

dogs had eczema and we used to bathe him in *Aquasept*. It worked wonders on him! I've heard *Aquasept* soap has been banned now – for whatever reason. A bit like "creosote", which preserved the wood but gave you cancer, so it wasn't any good. The new soap that replaced *Aquasept* is rubbish.

After showering in *Aquasept*, I had to take a mouth wash, again to avoid infection. My mouth was all burned from the radiation treatment. I had terrible mouth ulcers and was slopping lots of bits of dead skin out of my mouth. I had to use this mouth wash, *Cortisol*, I think it was called. It seemed like a mix of napalm and acid and because I had all these sores in my mouth, this stuff was a nightmare to use. It felt as though it was burning my mouth. It was so painful! I've since used the stuff with no ulcers in my mouth and it still burns. It brought tears to my eyes, but because the medics told me it had to be done three times a day, I stuck with it. The radiation caused me to constantly have a dry mouth and subsequently, split lips. It also caused my tear ducts to dry out and I still take drops for my eyes twenty years on.

I had tremendous piles, and Dr Hutchison who was the consultant responsible for my transplant insisted on having a look at these piles. Dr Hutchison was a strange guy. He was supposed to be one of the God Squad but he seemed very interested in my arse, since he always wanted to check out my piles and stick his fingers round about it. To be fair, he did give me morphine to reduce the pain of my piles. Or maybe he just wanted to send me off to sleep while he got a better fiddle!

I want to have a little bit of a dig at architects, but not a serious one.

I live just outsider Leicester but I'm in the town quite often for hospital appointments. Now, Leicester is one ugly town. I'm sure it was lovely before the town planners decided that all the old buildings should be knocked down and that architects would be hired to design stuff. All I see now in all these towns that have destroyed their lovely old buildings are bland concrete blocks, on concrete stilts, usually. I wonder if the architects get their kids to design these buildings? Submit the kids' plans and pocket the money. It seems to me that little thought has gone into the buildings. They are ugly, grey, and unfriendly. Also, the windows are filthy.

Another different thought. When you take tablets, you get negative side effects. Why don't you get positive side effects? Why have I not developed a 6-pack or have the body of Adonis? Instead, I get the shits, or bunged up, headaches – all due to side effects of the tablets I'm taking. You'd think by now that someone would have done something to give you a little bit extra benefit. Naw! Glaxo Smith Kline, you've got to try harder.

I think my first meal post-transplant was baked potato, baked beans and little pork sausages. I don't think I ate much.

During those three weeks, the hospital decided to have a last throw of the dice, as it were, and sent me to The Queen Elizabeth Hospital in Birmingham to see a liver specialist. I was treated by a guy called Dr Mutimer, who was Australian. He had a bit of a sense of humour and joked that I wouldn't be getting drunk this New Year because my liver was already buggered. Aussie sense of humour, you might say! At this point, I was a fluorescent yellow, felt like shit and was really itchy all over, which is another story. The Doctor took me of all the tablets I'd been on and over the period of two or three days without any tablets my liver started to improve. Following this, and the blood plasma transfusion, my biliruben count slowly reduced from the count of 1050.

While I was in The Queen Elizabeth, I was in a mixed ward, which was really awful. The nursing staff were horrible: cruel and disinterested in their work with patients. I'd had a cannula inserted into my arm, which never felt right from the minute it was put in, but we persisted with it. Very soon after, the cannula blocked and over time, I asked various nurses if they could remove it. Due to lack of confidence in the early days of my trips to hospital I found it hard to ask the medical staff for help. But now, I would just kick off and pull the cannula out by myself! However, back then I was a bit slow, as after thirty-six hours of my first asking the nurses to remove the cannula, with my arm the size of a football, they eventually attended to my request. Thank you very much - horrible bastards!

Then, a female patient in the bed opposite me started screeching, "I've had an accident!" in her Brummie voice, "I've had an accident!"

And boy, when it hit our nostrils, had she had an accident! She'd obviously crapped herself and it was absolutely stinking! Fortunately, I had a couple of oranges in my bag and Sophie said, "Peel an orange, quick!"

I did this and Sophie shared the peel between us. At her suggestion, we rubbed the orange peel hard between our hands and then put our hands to our noses. All we could smell was orange – a much better fragrance! This poor woman was trying to get the nurses' attention and all the while the nurses ignored her. When the nurses did eventually attend to the patient, they spoke to her in a very derogatory way, making her feel awful. They were not nice.

The food was not only unappetising but it was dumped down in front of each patient – usually just out of reach! I remember one night being 'served' sole for my evening meal and it was so over cooked that it was difficult to cut. Bearing in mind that I was very unwell and could hardly feed myself anyway, I would have appreciated a hand from a nurse to cut my food, but there was no help forthcoming. I had to just leave this meal, and several others, and go hungry frequently.

I was then moved to a little side ward in the Queen Elizabeth. It was a four bed ward and opposite me was a black guy – an Afro-Caribbean – and next to me was an Indian. When the Indian chap left the side ward, the Afro-Caribbean guy would say to me, "I fuckin' hate these pakis! They're dirty bastards!"

And when the black guy disappeared out of the ward, the Indian guy would say, "See these dirty black bastards? They are lazy, drug-taking so-and-so's."

I thought to myself, "I'm glad I can't get out of here, or both these guys will be saying, 'See these white guys, they're complete shits!' Or whatever other negative comments they might want to make!

The papers report that white people are racist, but it seems to me that whatever colour or creed you are, you hate everybody else. That's the impression I got in that little side ward, anyway.

The situation in the ward got so bad between poor nursing and unappetising food that I decided I was coming home. Sophie and I put this suggestion to the nurses, who in turn spoke to Dr Mutimer, who said, "We'll get your care transferred back to Leicester and they can administer the blood plasma infusions."

So that's what we did. I was very glad to get away from the Queen Elizabeth Hospital.

Daniel, Sophie's brother, who lived in Birmingham at the time, offered to come and collect me from The Queen Elizabeth Hospital. Now, Dan was very young at the time and a bit of a boy-racer. There are some bad underpasses, with bad bends between Birmingham and Leicester, and Dan was taking the bends at about 70mph. He banged against the kerb and his car went from one side of the road to the other. I said, "Bloody hell, Dan, I'm going to a lot of trouble as it is trying to live. I don't want you trying to fucking kill me!"

Before being treated at Leicester Royal, it was arranged that I'd spend a few days at home over Christmas. We spent Christmas Day at Sophie's mum's house. Joyce, her husband Dave and my favourite niece, Sally, came down from Scotland and we all spent Christmas together, which was lovely. Sophie and her family all chipped in and bought me a lovely aviator jacket that year for Christmas

– really nice. Everybody had bets on me to die and they were each hoping to get my jacket. I'm not joking! They even bought the jacket three sizes too big so that it could possibly fit Dan. I'm not joking! But I'm still here, and I still have my jacket! It's got patina with age!

I never was in any doubt about the transplant being a success. I always believed that it would work. I absolutely expected great things of the transplant. I expected to go in there, have my transplant, be ill, recover, get better and lead a normal life. I can't remember the medical staff telling me anything other than I would be really sick and lose all my hair – I knew all that. But, I naively thought that once I'd been cured, that would be it. I would go back to what I was health-wise, five years previously. But it wasn't like that. In reality, I don't think all the horrible side effects and all the nasty things that could go wrong were ever really discussed with me. No. I didn't feel let down entirely. I was feeling shite. I was too busy being ill to be thinking about anything else.

During my recovery following my transplant, Sophie's brother, Keith, who is a good baker, used to baked lovely cakes and biscuits among other things and bring some to me in hospital. He was also quite fond of cannabis. He thought he'd cheer me up one day and put a bit of cannabis in the biscuits he'd brought to me in hospital. I didn't have much of an appetite and had no idea what Keith had done, so I had been passing the biscuits around the nurses. The nurses were taking the biscuits two or three at a time and they were all quite giggly and happy. No wonder – they were Space Cookies!

I was in hospital for a relatively short period, I think, after my transplant. Then I had a four month period when I continued to get well and then the GVH (Graft Versus Host) flared up, which is where the body tissue rejects the transplant tissue, when it's not quite compatible. The doctors had no choice but to go ahead with a match that wasn't quite compatible, since my own cells couldn't be used because they were riddled with cancer, so they tried to match up as best they could. The only time a match is completely compatible, I think, is if you have an identical twin. To resolve the problem, the immune system is pegged back to try to minimise damage caused by the GVHD. I never returned to peak fitness after my transplant because I'd had total body radiation – a bit like the Chernobyl disaster. It was like nuclear fall-out. That's what I was suffering from.

My first beer after my transplant was, I remember, when Joyce and Dave were down to see me. I don't know if I'd just got out of the hospital for the afternoon or if I'd got home for good, but I really fancied a beer. My sister was quite reluctant, due to her concerns about my health. Dave was up for it of course, so we went to the Manchester, which was my local, round in Sheridan Street. My sister relented and bought me a half pint of Tetley's! It tasted great!

Chapter 10

I then started getting all these GVH attacks, and the
doctors put me on different kinds of immuno-suppressants
to try to stop the GVH. This was when the liver and
kidney failure started – all were additional health problems
post-transplant, things I hadn't been told could happen,
might happen, or would happen. I was no sooner out
of the transplant experience, than I was facing another
difficult experience. I was out of the frying pan, into the
fire and it's kind of been like that throughout. I was only
six months post-transplant when I had the liver and kidney
failure, which they ultimately put right but I had to go to
Queen Elizabeth 11 Hospital in Birmingham to see the
Liver Specialist there. He took me off all the immuno-
suppressants I was on. It wasn't as scary as it might have
been to come off them, as the specialist in Birmingham
told me that it was the immuno-suppressant tablets
causing all the trouble with my liver and kidneys.

Norman: Following this appointment I was sent to
Birmingham to meet with a Liver specialist – was it
Dr Mutimer – a Consultant. I was suffering from an
excruciating itch inside my whole body which was
worse than having the transplant. I was sent for a
blood plasma transfusion. Dr Mutimer stopped some
of my "liver medication" that had been prescribed by
Hutch - Mr Hutchison, my Consultant at Leicester

Royal and a liver transplant was talked about as a possibility.

Sophie: And you could hardly eat.

Norman: I survived on Bovril and onion rings!

Dr Hutchison at Leicester Royal was responsible for putting me on the immuno-suppressants. Unfortunately my body responded in a way that was most unusual, and normally only affects one person in thousands, so Dr Hutchison wasn't expecting this to happen. Also, because I had this GVH, Leicester had to try to do something and the course of action they chose, unfortunately, didn't suit me. By the time the doctors realised what was going on, I was critically ill again.

I spent time in Birmingham Hospital. Dr Mutimer, an Australian, was lovely, as were all the doctors I saw. However, I found the behaviour of the other staff in the hospital appalling. I felt that while there were a lot of good doctors and nurses there was also a significant minority of nurses who seemed to be in the job only for the money, and the less they could do, the happier they were. I felt that was the case of some staff at all levels – from top to bottom.

I am fortunate that 1) I have the sort of personality that won't put up with it and 2) my wife will sort them out, and she has done on a number of occasions. I think it is important to have someone like Sophie. I feel really sorry for people in hospital if they don't have a voice and nobody is listening to them. The patient in hospital is very vulnerable. Sometimes doctors can talk over a patient, as if the patient isn't there. Although that has rarely been my experience, if medical staff have that attitude or rudeness with me, I just give back exactly the same. For example, if they are trying to be smart or show off in front of their colleagues and ask me questions about my condition, I just reply by saying, "Refer to the notes." It quickly shuts them up!

Fortunately, I've never been so unwell that I've needed someone else to feed me.

If I was to compare the ability of the staff in a specialist ward with the staff in the general ward, the staff in the specialist ward tended to be better at their job. I have never been treated badly in a specialist ward, but occasionally you will meet a bad nurse on the specialist ward. When I've felt I've not been treated appropriately, I tell them. I say whatever I want to say. I don't know if the nurses are overworked or overwhelmed, but if I complain, although they don't like being told, they don't take it out on me. I'm sure the medical staff would prefer it if patients would just sit there and be passive, but I won't do that.

When my liver problem was sorted out, I said to Hutch, the Consultant at Leicester Royal, involved with my bone marrow transplant, who put me on those drugs that affected my liver, "I appreciate that you saved my life once, but I want you to recognise that you almost lost it too! I think we're now at 15-all!"

In about February, the medics thought they had got me well enough to be transferred back to Leicester Royal from the Queen Elizabeth Hospital in Birmingham. I was to have regular blood plasma infusions at Leicester every day. I walked from home in Sheridan Street to the hospital daily, for bags of plasma, and one day towards the end of treatment, I was caught short midway home. I minced my way down the road for a couple of hundred yards or so, pinching my buttocks together, then I shuffled. But all to no avail – I shat myself!

I got home and thought "Thank goodness for jogging trousers with elasticated ankles!"

I used to go up to the hospital and sit for about four hours while this plasma went through, as a blood derivative, I suppose. It was here that I met John and Elaine Gamble. I was so jaundiced and yellow that John and Elaine thought I was a Scottish Pakistani! Elaine told me that she and John used to say they could never have imagined a Pakistani would have such a broad Scottish accent, and they thought it was really funny. John was also attending the hospital for treatment for Lymphoma. Nice bloke. He was a farmer. I only knew John for about three months before he passed away, but Elaine, John and I got on really well and spent a lot of time together at the hospital. It was really sad. I was in hospital the night he died and Elaine came and told me. That was upsetting. John wasn't the first person I'd met in hospital who had died, though. Death, it seems, is just part and parcel of life.

I've remained great friends with Elaine, and she has helped Sophie and me out on numerous occasions. At one point she had bought a house off the farm, giving the main farmhouse to her stepson, but when she knew Sophie and I needed a house, she delayed moving into her new home and lent it to us for about four months! It was really kind of her to do that, and in appreciation, we decorated her new home before we left. Sophie and I remain friends with Elaine to this day and we see each other quite regularly.

I'd been encouraged to meditate by both my Kung Fu and Karate instructors and to try to find my inner Chi. I was in bed one night in Sheridan Street, post-transplant, doing my meditation and breathing, when – as strange, unlikely or unbelievable as it might seem – I feel as if I left my physical body. What happened was that I was thrust through this tunnel of cloud or white light into complete blackness. This complete blackness is where people's energy and spirit goes when you're asleep, when you've meditated, left your body or when you die. Your energy then goes somewhere else – the Indians call it Nirvana. I don't know. It felt as if I could connect with people, like my parents, my dogs, friends who'd died. I had no words or conversation with anyone I saw but I could read the energy, and it could read you. You could summon people's energy or the energy of trees, plants and flowers, which could all be seen vividly. It seemed as if you could paint a picture of wherever you wanted to be and the energy would be there! Your energy just went somewhere into the ether, if you like, but you could still connect – just in a very different way. You could just think of someone and they would come up, or they could think of you and you would go to them. It lasted for about two minutes and during that time I touched base with everybody I knew who was no longer alive. I felt that I was touching other people's spirit or soul – call it what you will. These people were not aware of me; their energy was there, and available to them, but they didn't seem to know how to control it or use it in order to reach the next level, as it were. Another impression I got was that people with negative energy – bad people – would never move into that place. Only good people would get there. For example, if you persistently lied, it felt, to me, that you'd soon be sussed and never make it. It seemed like a real, feel-good factor sort of thing. There was no sign of a God, and no need to be religious.

But something disturbed me and interrupted the experience, because in no time at all, I was back down the tunnel and back in my bed. I felt euphoric at the time, because it was a real eye-opener and it made me think that maybe there *is* something after death. Just not in the way that religion spouts it.

It only happened to me once, and once only. I wasn't on tranquillisers, or painkillers, or any other mind-altering drugs. Take it as you will.

Sophie: ...and we had the most dreadful night. It was just awful. I had made some arrangements for you coming home. The hospital hadn't, but I had. I went to the GP and got them to buy us a sats probe to measure your oxygen concentration, so at least we would know what oxygen you had going round in your body when you were at home. It cost £300 but it's been worth every penny and we've still got that sats monitor, which we still use. It's helpful. And I'd also told the GP that we were worried about you coming home without any oxygen, so would it be okay to have a cylinder at home on stand-by, just in case it was needed? And he said he thought that was entirely reasonable, and he gave me the practice cylinder.

Norman: It was half empty anyway.

Sophie: It was half empty, but there was some in it, just to use in case of an emergency. So I brought you home, propped you up in bed, and waited to see what would happen. You had a reasonable evening, but by night-time, you were in a complete state. Your sats were very low, you were very panicky and couldn't breathe, and you really weren't feeling well at all. So we had a chat about what the options were: getting the emergency GP, which we thought was probably a waste of time; or going to A&E, which we thought was probably taking your life in your hands.

When I got home after being discharged I told Sophie that I was struggling and didn't know how I was going to manage at home. We stayed at home for a couple of hours, but then returned to the hospital where I was readmitted. The surgeon who had said I was fit to go home was Greek – I thought he was quite an arrogant person who had made a wrong decision on my account.

Sophie: So we kept you on the oxygen the GP had given us, overnight, and then first thing in the morning, at 8 o'clock, I rang the ward that had discharged you and told them, "He's not well enough to be at home and I'm bringing him back!" They were not very happy, but I didn't give them a choice. So I took you back, in your pyjamas and your dressing gown, to that ward. They were still not happy, but you clearly weren't well enough to be at home, and they found a space for you on the medical ward. There you had some bronchoscopies: a camera put down into your tubes of your lungs. They also did some washings for infection, and that's when they found out that you'd got this multi-drug-resistant chest infection. You had to have several bronchoscopies during the course of your treatment on that ward, downstairs, in the two bedded room, with the guy with lung cancer.

Yeah. So they treated you with antibiotics, and you were there a while, weren't you? Did you have some physiotherapy and stuff?

Norman: Can't remember.

Sophie: Think you did. Anyway, you were there for a few weeks, not feeling…

Norman: I remember the ward being dirty.

Sophie: Yeah.

Norman: There was shit all over the walls.

Sophie: Yeah. And… some of them were all right on that
            ward.

Norman: Ward 15.

I spent fourteen weeks in total in The Glenfield Hospital.
As weeks went by and my condition improved, I often
got up and got dressed into ordinary clothes, and on one
such day Joyce and Ian had come down from Edinburgh
to visit me and we sneaked out for a curry without any of
the hospital staff knowing! Very bad. Joyce was panicking
in case we got caught! Must say, we had a great curry at
my favourite haunt, The Raj, owned by a good guy called
Khan. Again, Joyce was crapping herself, because I had
just wandered off without telling anyone. It's often the best
way, because it saves the staff panicking.

Sophie: And eventually, it was decided that you could
            come home, but you would need to bring oxygen.
            So you had some physio and OT assessments, and
            they decided to send you home with a package of
            care and some oxygen. And when you came out of
            hospital, you were as frail as you've ever been, really.

Norman: Why was I never… Why was I feeling so much worse
            after I came out? I mean, okay, I can accept that I
            wouldn't be as good, maybe, but it just seemed to
            go from some difficulty breathing to almost nothing

overnight. Why is that?

Sophie: Well, I suppose it was a combination of both of your lungs collapsing, and the surgery, because you had to have the other stuck back, in the end, didn't you? Oh, I'll tell you what! You had talc on the other one. You had a reaction to it, didn't you? A quite severe allergic reaction.

Norman: It was painful.

Sophie: Yeah.

Norman: I'm surprised you didn't hear me screaming from home. It really burnt from the inside out.

Sophie: That's right. They were quite concerned that you'd had a severe allergic reaction to the second lot of talc on the left lung.

Norman: That was like… it was like I was being chemically burnt from the inside out. It felt like I was literally on fire, burning. It was incredibly painful, and I was screaming. I couldn't help it, it was… And I think in the end I got about 40 mls of morphine, which basically knocked me out.

Sophie: Yes. I remember you did tell me that you'd had to have a big dose of morphine because of the pain from the talc. And I remember one of the doctors

telling me they thought you had a severe allergic
reaction to it, because it was the second time you'd
had it.

So where did we get to? Why you'd become much,
much more short of breath. And I suppose that's a
combination of Graft Versus Host disease and the
acute injury that you had to your lungs. Because that
chest infection you had was severe, severe enough to
collapse both of your lungs. And, I suppose that kind
of thing leaves a lot more scarring behind, so your
lungs would have been a lot more stiff during that
episode, because you were very, very ill. I suppose
it was just a result of the healing from that, and the
scarring from the infection.

Chapter 11

December 1996 was the first Christmas Sophie and I had at home – and it was fab. We went to Bradgate Park on a beautiful, cold, frosty, clear day to walk Samson and Sasha, our dogs. On our return our goose was cooked!

When I got out of hospital after my stem cell transplant, I started a photography course – just a simple introductory course. Someone else who'd been up at the Transplant Unit subscribed to a photography magazine and had left a whole lot of magazines lying on the coffee table in the sitting room/waiting room at the Unit. These magazines were pretty much soft porn. All the photographs were of scantily clad women and Dr Hutchison who was a real god-fearing man was disgusted at the fact that someone would leave this sort of literature lying around his waiting room. Of course, because I'd said I was doing a Camera Course, I got the blame for bringing in the magazines. Not guilty!

In 1998, I developed cataracts in both eyes. I thought I was going blind – it was a very scary feeling. I was referred to the Ophthalmology Department, and saw Miss Bibby, the Consultant, who reassured me that I only had cataracts and that my eyesight would be ok after the operation. The operation was carried out on each eye, one week apart. My eye was very painful following the operation. We thought it was either a stitch left in my eye or the stitch had not dissolved or I had scar tissue. Despite the discomfort – it was great to see again!

Around this time, we'd booked a holiday in Orkney. We loaded the Volvo and Sophie and I travelled there with Sophie at the wheel as my eye was giving me a lot of grief. On the Orkney Ferry, a girl leaned on our Volvo and asked us for a light, so we obliged from the car ciggy lighter. She got into conversation with us and asked why we were going to Orkney. When we said we were going there on holiday, she was incredulous that we should choose Orkney and concerned that we would be there for a whole week. So she gave us a large block of cannabis to help us get through it!

We stayed at a campsite, and pitched our tent. The night was freezing cold but it is a beautiful island and spotlessly clean – probably because everything is blown into the sea. My eye continued to give me grief, so on my last night I enjoyed several nips of Highland Park whisky and half a block of cannabis – and had the best sleep I'd had all holiday!

On my return, I visited the doctor, who removed the leftover stitch from my eye – what a relief – and all was well with my sight.

After Sheridan Street, we moved to a detached house in the North of Leicester, Avebury Avenue. It was really run down. An old woman had lived in it, and it had been basically untouched for what seemed like forty or fifty years. The house needed re-plumbing, rewiring, central heating – in fact, everything really. We got on with the job, built a garage on the side of the house and tidied up the garden. The garden was so overgrown that when I cut the grass back I found a greenhouse, a rotting old shed and a pond! I grew tomatoes!

There was this old lean-to conservatory at the back of the house which we repaired and double glazed where necessary. We put on a new door, laid Victorian quarry tiles on the floor and housed our plants in there. Trevor's wife, Linda, came to visit with her son Harry who was about four years old at the time, and he was playing in the back garden with our dogs. Unknown to us, Harry had taken the outside hose, dragged it into the conservatory and turned the tap on. Our brand new, freshly painted, tiled and furnished conservatory became a swimming pool. I insisted that Linda kick Harry's arse, but she preferred to deal with the incident verbally!

When you get cancer, it's a big shock, and obviously during my treatment when I was unwell, I went on the dole. You get such a paltry amount! I often wonder how people with fewer resources than I had, manage, actually, because I had Sophie and she had a bit of money coming into her from her dad's pension. Before I met Sophie, Trevor took the reins – he was always working if I wasn't, so we always got the mortgage paid and the lodger's rent helped with costs. It was a bit close sometimes, but it was never desperate. It makes me wonder, though – if a man goes in to hospital for treatment and is the main breadwinner, how does he make ends meet? He's had his treatment, he's at home and he's not able to do much. Also, his wife maybe needs to take a month or two off work to look after him, so she's probably not getting paid. Especially if they have kids, they still need money coming in. How do they do it? They must be getting help from their family. This situation is just so wrong. If you're born in Afghanistan, or Iraq and places like that, or if you're a charity, the government are giving money away; while there are people in Britain who have cancer and other chronic illnesses, worrying about how they are going to pay their rent or mortgages, with not enough help from the government. How can that be right? I don't know enough about it but it seems like it needs addressing.

I just thought I'd have a rant.

At some point, when I was about thirty five years old, I decided that I was going to get my back tattooed. I knew what I wanted, but I never saw a design anything remotely like it. So I made a collage of all the things I wanted, sort of cobbled it together, and took it to the tattooist who drew it properly. We just tweaked it here and there and then we started to get my back tattooed. I went for a whole back covering of tattoos. Well, well, well! Twenty two hours– obviously not all in one go – and a shedload of money later, I had my back done. The art work is an oriental, Japanese theme. It turned out alright. I was pleased with the result. The tattooist had been at the job for weeks when he confessed that this was the first whole back piece he had ever done. Prior to getting the tattoo done, I was telling someone about my plan and said who the tattooist was. The person I was telling replied the tattooist was a cocaine addict! Addict or not he did a good job!

I remember Dr Hunter being less than impressed, but what do you do, eh? It was my back!

One day in 2000, my job was to pick up steel tubes from a place called Hub-Le-Bas. I was driving up the A52 towards Boston and I turned left at the roundabout onto a long straight road, driving at 40mph. A car, far off in the distance, was overtaking a long line of cars, driving towards me. I kept thinking he'd pull into the various gaps between cars that were available to him. Alas – he chose not to pull in and smashed into my lorry. The driver of the car died instantly. At the inquest an open verdict was returned. The agency I was driving for that day was called Solutions. They didn't pay me for that particular shift because I hadn't delivered the goods!

Following the accident I received an insurance payout for Psychological Trauma of approximately £13,000.

Due to the chemotherapy/radiotherapy I'd previously received, my teeth had been affected and literally had gone soft and crumbly. I chose to use the payout to part fund my £20,000 dental implant bill.

Norman: On top of this, the radiotherapy shrank my gums to the point where there was no enamel covering my teeth. Because I had such a sweet tooth at the time, my teeth basically just rotted – well, it seemed to me overnight. Despite the fact that I had to clean my teeth after I'd ate everything.

Sophie: You had no saliva, that's why.

Norman: I had no saliva as well, which…

165

Sophie: From radiotherapy.

Norman: …from the radiotherapy, and that obviously made
                my mouth very dry. And again, any sugars that
                attached themselves to the teeth were stuck there
                for longer periods. So my dentist came up with
                the bright idea of dental implants. I had just been
                involved in a road traffic accident, where the guy
                that forced me off the road subsequently died, and
                I was sort of suffering from post-traumatic stress. I
                got a payout of £13,500, which basically was put into
                my dental work. I could have dental implants, which
                have been absolutely fantastic.

                The dental implants involved pulling out my teeth,
                me being gummy for about six months till they
                healed up; then having my gums cut open again,
                and titanium pegs drilling and screwed into my jaws,
                upper and lower. Again, you've got to wait until
                these heal up, and then you can be fitted for false
                teeth, which are actually physically screwed onto the
                pegs, so that your teeth look as real and as natural
                as anybody else's. And I have to say, they've been
                absolutely fantastic, and my self-esteem went up no
                end when I was able to smile again. Not that it was
                a hardship for me not to smile, I should add, but if I
                wanted to smile, I could.

In 2003 I was driving for a company called Christian
Salvesen. I returned to their depot after completing my

run and went to the fuel island to fuel up. It was pitch black at night and none of the lights were working on the fuel island. I filled up my lorry with diesel but I didn't see that there was a fairly high kerb. I stepped off it blindly and jarred my bi-lateral prosthetic hips very badly. I crawled to the Christian Salvesen office, filled out an accident report form, and went to my GP the next day who referred me to the orthopaedic surgeon. I was x-rayed. Fortunately, there was no damage to my hips, but I'd torn ligaments and was signed off work for six weeks. Eighteen months later, Christian Salvesen paid out £2,300 in damages, which I also put towards my dental bill.

Norman: To get the rest of my teeth finished, we put some money towards that, and I went through the whole procedure again, to get the gaps filled in, as it were. I had dentistry work to the tune of about £20,000 – £16,000 of which was paid for via other monies, and the rest we put in ourselves. But I have to say that it made such a huge difference, just like having my sight restored, it was truly a wondrous thing. It was marvellous to eat food properly and to not be mumbling or slurring my words, because I had no teeth, it was great. Fantastic. So yeah, I'm glad I had it done.

Another driving incident I really got my teeth into was when I was driving for Samworth Bros, and had been given a little 7.5 ton lorry to take meats to Kent. I got as far as Hemel Hempstead when I saw a German Shepherd dog running down the embankment, across the motorway in front of an articulated truck! The driver did well to miss the dog. The dog was running southbound in the fast lane on the motorway! I pulled into the fast lane and drew up alongside the dog, grabbed her by the scruff of the neck and dragged the dog into my little truck. All the other drivers were rubber-necking, watching the situation! The dog wagged her tail and was as good as gold sitting in the passenger's seat beside me. I called the police and told them the story. They said they would check for any enquiries regarding a missing dog. We drove on down to Kent to deliver the goods.

On my way back to Samworth's Depot, Sophie collected the dog and took her home, but she was aggressive towards our dogs. I phoned the dog warden in Hemel Hemstead and explained the situation, and they told me that a farmer had reported that he'd lost a dog fitting this one's description. My details were passed onto the farmer who then came to our house to confirm the dog was his – which it was. The dog was called Crumble! He took his dog home and sent me flowers, with thanks!

We've certainly done some renovations in our time. We lived in and renovated Sheridan St, then moved to Avebury Avenue and did that house up. Then moved in with Elaine and redecorated, and then moved to Stoke Golding in 2003.

Brooke House in Stoke Golding was a lovely country house – quite big – four bedrooms and three large reception rooms, with a fairly big kitchen. However, the garden was pretty tiny. For that reason I was never that keen on the house. The old lady who owned it had just died and her daughter had cleaned the house and given everything a coat of magnolia paint before selling it. It looked as though the house was in move-in condition. Oh, how wrong!

We saw the house and bought it, but when we were ready to move into it we noticed that the pipes had been leaking, the attic and ceilings were all stained, brand new sockets and switches had been put on top of old wiring and the central heating was poor. The more you scratched the surface, the more this house fell apart. Another renovation job! I started with the rewiring and Sophie's brother Keith did the plumbing, including the fitting of a second-hand oil fired Raeburn cooker we'd bought. It took six people to carry the Raeburn stove off the lorry and into position, then Keith connected it up. I painted the outside of the house white. It had horrible aluminium framed windows which I rubbed down, then I masked off the windows and painted them white, and that made a huge difference. We got the front of the house paved with mono-block. We went to town on improving this house!

We had a little en-suite built in one of the bedrooms in Stoke Golding – with a shower, a little sink and a toilet, but because it was miles away from the drains, we had to use a macerator. The macerator stopped working one day, so I phoned up the chap who had installed it to let him know the situation. He came to the house straight away and unearthed a pair of Sophie's drawers out of it. What a laugh! No wonder the macerator wasn't working! How her knickers got down there, is anybody's guess!

We had no immediate neighbours, although there was a farm nearby. I approached the farmer and asked if he would sell me a little bit of his field to make my tiny garden bigger. His wife came across as a miserable cow and was having none of it. Her youngest son was just as bad, but the eldest son was a pleasant guy and would always speak. They had a Rottweiler dog that roamed about the road, and people would bring it to my door and have a go at me for letting it roam! I'd explain that it wasn't my dog and belonged to the farm, but they couldn't see the farm as it sat in a dip down the farm lane.

Later, in December 2006, we moved on again, to Hunts Close, Botcheston – another renovation job. We got professionals in this time – joke! Seriously, though, we always chose to buy properties that required renovating, because it meant we could get houses that we wouldn't otherwise have been able to afford.

We discovered that one of Sophie's colleagues lived in Stoke Golding village. I got friendly with her partner, Simon; we'd go for a few beers together – too many, usually! – and we got in with the local crowd. It was fine. I quite liked my time in Stoke Golding. Sophie and her colleague, Katie, were working in Boston, Lincolnshire, at the time, staying there during the week and coming home at weekends. Their accommodation in Boston was abysmal: filthy, with equipment that didn't work, cockroaches – just awful. The block of flats looked like a Russian Gulag. It got so bad that Katie actually resigned from her position. I admired her for doing that. I think you have got to stick up for yourself. Sophie stuck it out, and Katie got a job elsewhere.

Katie and Simon's wedding was in 2007. We were good mates with them and we got an invitation to their wedding. They had a beautiful wedding in a lovely stately home and they did this marvellous thing: having endless free champagne. After the ceremony, I think I spent most of the day chasing after waiters and waitresses looking for free top-ups! It was a great day and the weather was lovely and warm. I think it was the last time I ever danced, as well, because after that day I really went downhill. We couldn't afford to stay in the stately home hotel where the wedding was held. It was £300 a night and we thought, 'bugger that!' so we stayed in a hotel in Market Harborough, nearby. It was an absolute flea pit – and I say this without joking – we were both eaten alive by the time we came down for breakfast in the morning. It was a crap ending to a great day – but we should have known better.

Chapter 12

My arthritis was playing up again at this point and I
noticed I was getting out of breath sooner than I normally
would. Trevor gave me a hand when he could but I was
getting fairly busy so I hired an apprentice. I took on a
young lad who had written to me asking if I could take on
an apprentice. I met with him and explained that I couldn't
pay very much, but if he was looking for experience he
could join the team, as it were. He had no transport but
said his mum would drop him off at mine in the morning
on her way into Leicester. The first day he was due to start
he was late, as his mother got lost. She was in a real panic
when she eventually dropped her son off, apologising,
saying it was her fault and not her son, Tom's. I said not
to worry and asked if she'd like a cup of tea, to which she
replied, "Oh no, what I need is a big stiff one!" Well, how
do you answer that? Tom was immediately red-faced, and
needless to say, I ribbed him about it later!

I remember when Tom started, we were driving past
Enderby village church and there was a big board that
said: "Is Jesus in your heart?"

I asked him, with a straight face, "Do you have Jesus in
your heart, Tom?"

And because he didn't know me, and thought I was
a serious Christian boss that he had to impress, he got
all flustered, "Er... well... sort of. Well," he explained,
"I do... um... I do go out carol-singing with my mum at

CHAPTER 12

Christmas time..."
   Poor Tom!

Norman: Okay. So when was the GVHD diagnosed in my
            lungs? And why is it so difficult to detect...?

Sophie: That's a really hard one to answer, but you'd been
            getting short of breath, hadn't you? Yes, it was
            quite insidious, actually. Not a very dramatic onset,
            really, and obviously associated with repeated chest
            infections, which became more frequent and more
            severe as time went on.

Norman: 2007. That was when it was diagnosed.

Sophie: Yes. You must have been referred to the respiratory
            physicians, and had some lung function tests, and
            they diagnosed it then. You were in hospital a fair
            bit with the chest infections. You know, it crept up
            insidiously, because you were okay to begin with: you
            could walk, but then you couldn't do stairs very well.
            And then you couldn't do slopes, and could only
            walk on the flat.

Norman: That's right. That was just prior to the collapse.

Sophie: Just prior to the lung collapse. When did we get Max
            and Duncan?

Norman: Four years ago, in 2008.

Sophie: It became worse in 2008…

Norman: It did.

Sophie: …because you wouldn't have got the dog, Max, if you hadn't been able to exercise him, would you?

Norman: No. I was still exercising Max up until my lungs collapsed.

Sophie: Yes. But you were a bit worse, because you could only walk him on the flat.

Norman: Yeah. I didn't like hills. It was very noticeable.

Sophie: Going up hills.

Norman: If I can remember right, I think it was quite noticeable going up that hill towards our hotel in Malta, whatever year we went to Malta.

Sophie: Can't remember. No, what year did your lung collapse?

Norman: December 2008.

Sophie: Was it really three and a half years ago? Goodness. So you were being treated for a severe chest infection at home, with Tazocin, again. And yeah, that's when it happened, isn't it? 14 December, 2008?

Norman: Well, the GVH was detected in 2007, so whether
            I was then referred to photopheresis treatment in
            Rotherham at that point then...

Sophie: Yes. you were, because I was worried that when you
            were in Glenfield for all that time, you weren't having
            your photopheresis. Gosh, doesn't time fly when
            you're having a nice time? Yeah. So you were sent for
            photopheresis when it became apparent that the
            steroids and things really weren't controlling your
            lung GVH.

Norman: Yeah. So what's photopheresis?

Sophie: Photopheresis is a treatment for anything to do
            with naughty T cells. T cells are a special type of
            lymphocyte, a white blood cell, and T cells are what
            cause Graft Versus Host disease. So what happens
            is, you go on a machine which cleans out and filters
            all your blood, and filters out the naughty T cells.
            So these cells are extracted from your blood and
            they're held in a sort of holding chamber inside this
            machine, if you like. They inject a drug which binds
            itself onto the T cells and is activated with UV light.
            Then, once the T cells have been treated with the
            drug and the UV light, they're put back into your
            body. So they're still there, and they're still kind of
            working, I suppose, as part of your immune system,
            but they're hopefully not causing the Graft Versus
            Host disease quite so badly as they used to before.

And you have that done two days every month, and
how long does each treatment take?

Norman: About three hours.

Sophie: About three hours. So that's what photopheresis is.

Norman: So the goals are to stop the GVH?

Sophie: Yes. To treat it, keep it at bay.

Norman: Right. Even with the photopheresis treatment, was
            my GVH always going to get worse?

Sophie: I don't know.

Norman: Okay.

Sophie: And I don't suppose anybody knows that. I suppose
            you're not ever going to make it better, with
            everything it's done to you... But it's to hold it at bay,
            or stabilise it or whatever. I have to say, I did wonder
            at the time if they'd known this treatment had been
            available... in the beginning – why didn't they give it
            to you straight off?

Norman: So was it available then?

Sophie: I don't know. Well, presumably. But it was a fair way
            into the problems with the lungs before you were

referred for it.

Norman: I think I was about 11 years post-transplant when we started. I remember Dr Taylor telling us both, when we went to see him, that he'd never done anything on anybody that had been post-transplant for so long.

Not long after we got Max I got another of my numerous chest infections around November 2008. I don't know why it wasn't picked up. Maybe because I didn't complain about it too much. I just thought it would go away itself. I don't know why I thought that, given my medical history. The chest infection turned into pneumonia and I had it all through November. The effect of it was that I was very out of puff, but because I wasn't in any pain I just carried on without checking it out. Anyway, one night in December when I was in bed I had a massive coughing fit and I experienced this awful pain in my back, high up on the right hand side. Immediately, I couldn't get breath. I shouted to Sophie, who, to her credit, got out of bed right away, which is really unusual! Anyway, Sophie come through to my room and asked me what was wrong. I couldn't tell her as I'd no breath to speak.

Sophie: So you did that, and I was fanning you to try and get you some fresh air, to try and work out what the matter was. I was trying to get you to tell me what was wrong, because I couldn't make head nor tail of what was going on. It became apparent pretty quickly that there was something seriously wrong, but I didn't know what it was, and we had to get you to hospital. You'd got no clothes on, and it was December, and it was pretty cold. I didn't want to take you in the car with no clothes on, so I managed to persuade you – and it did require some persuasion, actually – to put some jeans and a tee-shirt on, and just slip some shoes on, because you didn't want to get dressed. You were all for going with no clothes on, because you were confused.

Norman: I was panicking.

Sophie: Yeah. Panicking and confused. So I managed to try and stay calm.

Norman: Horrible suffocating.

Sophie: I know.

Of course, I started to panic because I felt as though I was suffocating to death. Sophie said "We need to get you to hospital!" and because of the lack of oxygen in my body, my bowels started to loosen and I remember thinking that I couldn't shit myself en route to the hospital. I'd rather die with clean pants than go to hospital with shitty ones and survive! I remember when I was young my mum was very insistent I had clean underwear on, just in case I got run over – just the way you're brought up, I suppose! Anyway, I insisted that I had to go to the toilet before I went anywhere else. Mission accomplished – but I was getting shorter and shorter of breath. We made it to the car. It was 3 o'clock in the morning.

Sophie: I'd managed to get us dressed, and pop you in the passenger seat. I'd given you a couple of puffs of your inhaler, which you refused to take, but just in case it was something reversible, I managed to get you to take your inhaler. And got you to hospital fairly quickly, because we went through just about every red light, I think there was about six I counted on the way.

Sophie was driving like a rally driver, ignoring the red lights, racing between two cars, so we got to A&E in record time. Sophie dropped me off at A&E on my own and for some reason, after driving like a maniac, decided to be a good, thoughtful citizen and went and parked the car out of anyone's way, despite our situation. Meanwhile, I'm inside A&E gasping for breath, but it was so hot in A&E I just had to get back outside. So, I crawled out and all the hospital staff in the vicinity were just looking at me. Their looks seemed to say, "Drunken bastard! Serves him right."

Sophie: Got you to hospital within about 15 minutes, because the traffic wasn't too bad, and fortunately, there was a space outside A&E, so I pulled up outside, and I have to say, driving you to hospital was probably one of the first mistakes I've ever made in my life. We should have just called an ambulance, although you can never tell how long it would have taken to get here. But I found a security guy, and managed to get a wheelchair. You had got out of the car at this point, and you were crouched down outside reception, virtually incoherent. Do you remember this? No.

When Sophie rejoined me after parking the car, she said to me, "What are you doing?"

I gasped in reply, "Too hot! Too hot!"

She went into the building and asked the porter if he would get her a wheelchair, which he duly did, then pushed it at her and walked away. Sophie helped me into the chair and got me into A&E. She said to the staff not to muck about as she thought her husband had a collapsed lung and was not in a good state.

Sophie: So I got you in the wheelchair, and then there was a huge queue for reception, and you were obviously getting worse and worse. So I walked in majors because I knew where it was. Had I not known where majors was, I don't really know what would have happened, actually.

Norman: What's majors?

Sophie: It's the main area in A&E where the nurses' station is and where the doctors work from, where they can see everything going on. It's not marked, but it's a door off reception, and obviously, because I work in that hospital, I know how to get into it from reception. So yeah, because you know what it's like trying to get through to an NHS receptionist. You're not allowed to jump the queue, and you can't possibly be that ill, and all this. So I walked in, I said, "I've got my husband in reception, he's very unwell, and there's a queue. Can we just come in?"

I managed to find a nurse and showed you to her, and she said, "Yes love, bring him in and we'll stick him in triage." And so she sort of said to the triage nurse, "Oh this man here..." Can you remember any of this?

Norman: They started to fuck about with ECGs and stuff.

Sophie: Yeah. She said to the nursing assistant, "Oh, can you do an ECG on this man?"

The nurses wheeled me into a side room and started to give me an ECG. Sophie advised that I wasn't needing an ECG and told them to get me straight into the emergency resuscitation area, which they duly did. The Doctor on duty that night had my situation sussed immediately. I could hear everything that was being said to me but I couldn't respond.

Sophie: And I was really cross, and I said, "Look, no, I don't want you to do that... just stick a sats probe on him."

181

And she looked at me, like, as if to say, "Don't tell me what to do," and I said, "Do it! Just stick a sats probe on him!" So she did.

Norman: Which measures the oxygen supply.

Sophie: Which measures your oxygen supply in the blood, and if you're fit and healthy, it should be above 97, really. Anyway, yours was 69. By this time, you were blue, and it was obvious to anybody with half a brain that you were very sick. So she put the sats probe on and your oxygen saturation was 69, and fortunately, she recognised that there was a problem. She went to get the staff nurse, who also saw there was a problem, and they took you straight through in the resuss area. So finally, we managed to... I'm sure this only took a matter of five minutes, but it seemed like...

Norman: Forever.

Sophie: ...forever, you know. Trying to get through that queue, trying to stop them doing an ECG, trying to get somebody sensible. They got somebody to come and see you straight away, and it was Katie who used to work with me, who is one of our house officers or SHO. She was very good, so I was quite pleased to see her, because she remembered me as well. So I told her that you were being treated at home for a severe chest infection. I told her your history, I said that you'd got this chronic graft versus host disease, and that the hospital had rung up that day and said that you'd got a fungal infection. I can remember saying to her, "This is a sudden onset thing, he's either got an overwhelming fungal infection of the lungs and has just completely gone downhill because of that, or the only other thing I can think is that he's had a PE, a pulmonary embolism, a blood clot to the lung, because this is just really sudden. And it's one of those two things I think."

Anyway, so Katie got her registrar and she rang ITU straight away, and they got the intensive care doctor to come down. So, in the meantime, they were getting you a chest x-ray, and the chest x-ray showed that one of your lungs had collapsed because of a pneumothorax, which can happen as a complication of a severe chest infection, it's a recognised complication. Alison was the registrar, Alison Brewer, and I know Alison really, really well, because we used to work together on the delivery suite. And when she poked her head round the curtains, I was so pleased to see her, because I thought, "Oh, thank goodness! It's somebody sensible, and competent, and somebody I can have a conversation with, who's on intensive care tonight." Because I thought there was a fair chance that they might not take you to intensive care, because you've got chronic lung problems, and your chance of surviving intensive care with chronic lung problems is fairly minimal.

So we were waiting for the chest x-ray report to come, and Alison was talking to you about going to intensive care, and about CPAP, which is a non-invasive form of ventilation. And she was saying that she was going to have a word with the consultant, and she was asking me about your normal state, the things that you can do and things that you can't do. I was talking with her in the corridor, and halfway through, it dawned on me that she was having this conversation with me to see if she was going to give you an ITU bed or not. And it was really chilling, actually, to realise that I was having this conversation with my colleague about you, and that they might not accept you. It was like a clunk, halfway through me saying, "Oh, well, he doesn't really manage the stairs very well," and her asking "How far can he walk?"

And I think she must have seen my face when that clunk happened, because she said to me, "It's Dr..." Oh God, who was it? He's a horrible bastard, "Dr X is on tonight," But she said, "Don't worry, I'm not going to ring him, I'm just going to accept Norman and I'm going to take the consequences in the morning."

For which I will be eternally grateful to Alison, actually, because if she accepted you without telling or asking the consultant, and he came in in the morning and found you there, with respiratory failure, she would get a lifetime's worth of bollocking, but she was going to do it.

Anyway, so while we were having this conversation, your chest x-ray result came back, and it showed that you didn't have an overwhelming fungal infection, you'd got a pneumothorax. So David, who was the senior registrar for A&E, came very quickly, and he very, very quickly and very competently put a chest drain in for you. In fact, I think before that, Katie had been struggling to do your arterial blood gas, so I did that for you. You did manage to stay quite still.

My oxygen sats were down to 69% which was no use, given that you get out of breath at 92% - so no wonder I was gasping! X-rays confirmed that my lungs had collapsed. The Doctor asked, "Are we cutting his t shirt off? Or do you want to pull it off, Norman?"

I heard Sophie exclaim, "It's his favourite T-shirt! You can't cut it!" She added, "It's his Bruce Lee T-shirt!" Somebody might want it!"

Anyway, Sophie whipped my T-shirt off and the Doctor stuck a hole in my side, got the air out of my cavity and the pressure was relieved off my lungs. It went from me having only a couple of minutes to live, to within the next minute, getting my oxygen sats back up to over 90%. I was sitting in a chair when they did all this. As soon as they'd finished, I needed to go to the loo again. I thought I'd shat myself, and was concerned for everyone else in the room, for obvious reasons. I managed to get to the loo and fortunately all was well in that department. I was then

taken up to the acute recovery ward.

Norman: What's arterial blood gas?

Sophie: It's a little needle in the artery of your wrist to get some of your arterial blood, to see how much oxygen and carbon dioxide you've got going round your system.

Norman: Okay.

Sophie: It's painful, but I gave some local anaesthetic. He put the chest drain in, I held your hand, and I talked you through what he was doing, and he did it really quickly. And as soon as you got your chest drain in…

Norman: I was out. I could hear what everyone was saying, but I could not respond. I was non-responsive.

Sophie: You were out. Yeah. That's right. But we talked to you, and you got it in, and virtually, within 30 seconds of it being in, and your lung being re-inflated, you came round.

Norman: And went to the toilet.

Sophie: And you perked up a bit, and you felt a lot better and we could talk to you. And the nurses who were on that night were very good, actually, in A&E and resuss, because I can remember I asked the sister for a 50 ml syringe to flush your peg with, because we'd obviously had to stop your peg feed and we'd not thought about flushing it. And she said, "Oh yes, if you don't flush that, it will block up, won't it? Yes, I'll get one for you straight away," and she did. She went straight away, and understood the reason why you needed it flushing. So they were good.

Norman: What were the subsequent…

Sophie: So what happened then, was that Alison stayed down, and arranged for you to go to the medical admissions unit, to be looked after there overnight, so that you could be taken to Glenfield in the morning. So you didn't need to go to intensive care. And you went to Glenfield the next day. What were you going to say?

Chapter 13

I remember the morning I woke up in the hospital after my right lung collapsed. As you can imagine, I was feeling a good deal better than I had been twelve hours earlier when I'd been admitted. I noticed that the chap in the bed across from me in the ward was awfully confused. I don't know if he had a drug problem or not, but he was behaving strangely. He was just a young lad and he kept trying to get out of bed. The nurse, who was rushed off her feet, poor woman, kept putting him back into bed. Then he went and shat himself. Again, the poor nurse was trying to deal with someone else so she came along and basically just stuck yards and yards of toilet paper down the back of the patient's trousers, basically to soak up the slop temporarily, and put him back into bed.

This guy wasn't for staying there, but he had a catheter in, which obviously went into his bladder and the bag was fixed to the bed. So he decided he was going to make a break for it and he ran 2.4 metres. I know this was the distance because of the ceiling tiles – they're 600cm x 600cm, and I could see the distance he got from his bed before he was pulled back by the pain, I imagine. I knew he had stretched his catheter 2.4 metres, which must have been incredibly painful, but what made it even better from a spectator's point of view was that he had collapsed over this young girl's bed, over her feet, and she, at this point, was screaming hysterically. His pyjama trousers had fallen down the minute he'd started his bid for freedom, so all this shitty toilet roll had unravelled the whole length of the ward. It was a six-bay ward – with three beds either side. That was really quite funny in a surreal, strange sort of a way. But how sore would that have been?

Norman: And what about the nose infections that I kept getting?

Sophie: Oh goodness, where do they fit into things? That's been an ongoing, low level, shitty, chronic problem for a very long time. What seems to happen is that you get this kind of build-up of debris at the top of your nose, which is low level infected, and smells very bad. And intermittently, it falls down and comes out through your nose, doesn't it? And it's like a solid lump of...

Norman: Snot.

Sophie: ... green, infected material.

Norman: Snot.

Sophie: Snot. But it's quite solid.

Norman: Yeah, difficult to pass down the nasal tubes.

Sophie: And painful. And you know, not life-threatening, not the end of the world, but really quite unpleasant.

Before they come out, your breath smells quite awful for a couple of days beforehand, so we always know when they're coming. I can remember trying to get help with this symptom on numerous occasions, going to the GP and them not being very impressed. Yeah, and at some point, you were referred to ENT, where you saw someone quite unhelpful who told you to sniff salty water up out of a saucer, which you were less than impressed with. But they didn't actually tell you what the diagnosis was, or what was wrong. So we thought if ENT was no use, and the GP wasn't going to be any help, you just had to soldier on with that one. But they were really quite troublesome at one point, actually. But fairly recently, you've been back to ENT, haven't you?

Norman: The GP referred me back. She was thinking that the nasal infections were starting the chest infections.

Sophie: Yeah, like a post-nasal drip. I'm sure she's probably right. And you did see somebody, was it Mr Bannerjee in the end? And he had a look, and what did he say to you? It was radiotherapy change.

Norman: Yes. He said I was producing a very small amount of very thick mucus that wasn't running down, running freely. It was just basically building up, and building up, to the point where it had nowhere else to go, other than out.

Sophie: Yeah. And did he say it was to do with radiotherapy?

Norman: I think he probably did, and he told me about a
           spray, just salty water again, but in a spray can. It was
           a much easier idea than trying to sniff it out of a
           saucer, and that has helped.

Sophie: Yeah. And the other helpful thing was actually
           getting some sort of explanation and diagnosis,
           because that really is what you want. So you've
           been much less troubled with the nasal lumps
           since you started using the salt water spray. So,
           it seems a shame, again, that you suffered with a
           quite unpleasant symptom, for many, many years,
           without any kind of explanation or treatment, when
           all that was needed was a spray you can buy from
           the chemist, with salty seawater in it. But anyway. So
           where did we get to?

Norman: Just talking about the infections on my chest, getting
           worse after the...

Sophie: Yeah. So 2008, you had recurrent chest infections
           which were being treated at home with quite potent
           intravenous antibiotics.

Norman: When did it become necessary to start me on the
           IVs rather than tablets? About 2007?

Sophie: Yeah, I'm thinking about 2007, because in 2007, when your chest had become quite bad, you'd become quite run down and quite poorly.

Norman: My lungs collapsed. My left, my right lung collapsed.

Sophie: Your right lung collapsed, yes.

Norman: So I've got air retention, and told you I couldn't breathe. You rushed me to hospital.

Sophie: I did.

Norman: Glenfield. What happened at Glenfield?

Sophie: You went to Glenfield the next day, to the respiratory ward, and the chest drain stayed in. It was doing its job, it was letting out the air from the hole that had been made in your lung from the infection, and they hoped was that the hole would just spontaneously seal up – that's often just what happens. So eventually, the chest drain wouldn't be needed, and they'd be able to remove it, and then you would just get better. But unfortunately, that didn't happen. They waited and waited, and it just wasn't happening. So you were transferred to the thoracic ward, which was upstairs, to see about having your lung stuck onto your chest wall.

Norman: And this is the talc treatment.

CHAPTER 13

After my stay in the recovery ward, I was transferred to the Glenfield Hospital which is the main Lung (Respiratory) Centre for Leicester. I was in there for a fortnight and actually doing quite well when my other lung collapsed. Again, the timing was related to me being at the toilet, trying to move my bowels. Great! I'd been on so much morphine to kill the pain where they'd cut me up, that the drugs had bunged me up. The strain of going for a crap basically caused my lung to tear – I think I even heard a tearing sound. I immediately got out of breath again, but I managed to walk back to the ward. There was no-one there except for a cleaner.

I said to the cleaner, "I think my lung's gone again," thinking she might go and find a medical person.

However, she said, "I don't know, I'm a cleaner." And just to prove the point, as if I might suggest she was lying, she misted the counter with some kind of spray and rubbed it with a cloth.

"Will you get me some help?" I asked her angrily.

She looked angrily back at me, but trotted off and got me some help.

Sophie: That's right. That's called pleurodesis. So you went
            to the thoracic ward, and they tried to put some
            talcum powder in your chest drain, to see if the
            inflammatory reaction the talcum powder would
            generate would stick your lung to your chest wall, so
            that your lung would stay expanded, and wouldn't
            collapse. But that didn't work. So then they tried a
            blood patch, where they take some of your blood

and put it through the drain into the space, to try and see if the stickiness of the blood will seal the lung to the chest wall, but that didn't work.

So then they decided that they would have to do surgery. They do a sort of keyhole surgery into the lung, called VATS – video assisted thoracoscopic surgery – and pleural stripping, which is when they strip away some of the linings of your lung and your chest wall, and stick them together that way. And did you have that done Christmas Eve? You did, didn't you? Yeah.

I don't think they'd appreciated just how badly infected you were until they got into surgery and put the camera in. They said there was a lot of pus hanging around. Well, you know, there was always going to be. And everything was very inflamed. So they did the surgery; you came back and because you had lots of chest drains, arterial lines and monitoring in HDU, you came back onto high dependency. You were okay; you did alright.

On this occasion when the Doctor cut holes in my other side, I was lying on my bed. He improved the situation, and with it, my breathing. However, my lungs never stayed fully inflated. So the medics used blood to stick my lungs to my diaphragm in my chest cavity, in the hope that when the blood dried, the lungs would remain inflated. However, despite their best efforts, that didn't work. They then suggested that they would try the same treatment again, but would use a substance called liquid talc. When the liquid talc comes in contact with your body tissue, it causes a chemical burn. So, when the diaphragm and the lung tissue come in contact with each other, they should, in theory, stick and heal together. The chemical burn is so very painful! I felt as though my body was on fire from the inside out. I was screaming in pain. I was given about 40mls of morphine – so that was nice. I saw pink elephants and fluffy bunnies!

After my lungs were talced up, Sophie was helping me to have a shower, because I was still very weak. I had a drain coming out the right hand side of my chest and when I sat down on the chair in the shower area, the tube got caught between the top of the chair and its leg. As I stood up from the chair, it pulled the tube right out of my chest. Sophie got the nurse who said, "Put a clean cloth on it and I'll go and get the Doctor."

The Doctor, who who was from the former Eastern Bloc, had no gloves on, and said he'd put the tube back in – which was fine, and would give me anaesthetic – fine. Then he started to open up the wound again, and it was so sore that I was shouting at him to stop! He didn't seem to believe that I was in so much pain, and was adamant that he'd given me enough anaesthetic! From that point on, I picked up a ghastly infection in the hospital – I don't know if it was because the Doctor wasn't wearing gloves. I also think doctors should listen to you if you say you are in pain. I then developed another infection, coughing up all sorts of lung crap that looked a bit like custard, and was treated for that.

I was looked after really well at Glenfield Hospital. The two nurses who really shone out were Maria, who was German, and Jane, who called herself 'Calamity Jane'. They were very decent human beings and really pleasant. They always took time to speak to me, which I appreciated. I told them both that I'd give them a mention in the book. So here it is – Maria and Jane – and thanks again for your nursing care. Ill health can be very isolating – even in hospital, surrounded by lots of people, so it makes a difference if people take time with you.

As I got a bit better I was moved to Ward 15. The ward was absolutely filthy. There was dirty toilet roll all over the toilets, and the nursing staff weren't interested in their work. For example, I shared a room with another bloke, who was dying from lung cancer and because our room was out of sight of everywhere, the nurses would come in, take our seats and just start gossiping or talking about Coronation Street to each other as though we, the patients weren't there – commonly known as skiving! I was on antibiotics for the infection I had and was due to be given my medication regularly. The time for dispensing my tablets had overrun by two hours. When the nurse came into my room, I mentioned to her that I hadn't had my medication. She replied by saying that it didn't really matter if I was a bit late in getting my medication. I was annoyed at her attitude and told her so. I also gave her all the reasons why I should have my tablets on time. She wasn't pleased. The staff in Ward 15 liked neither me nor Sophie, because we had made so many complaints. As

I say, it went from many really good wards in Glenfield Hospital to Ward 15, where I felt the standard of care was much lower.

As time passed, I was informed by the Doctor during his medical round that I was fit to go home, which surprised me, as I wasn't feeling great at all. Anyway, I packed my bags and was discharged later that day.

Sasha hadn't been very well prior to me going into hospital. German Shepherd dogs are prone to getting trapped nerves in their back, through arthritis and other things. The effect of this is that the dog can't feel that their bowels are full, and they just start to poop without knowing it. Sasha was a very clean dog and it distressed her to turn round and realise what had happened. Because I was in hospital and in no position to help, we made the decision to put Sasha to sleep. Obviously I wasn't able to go with her and was very upset that we had to let Sasha go. We lost Sasha just before Christmas 2008. She was the mum of our eleven pups and was just over thirteen years old, which is a respectable age for a big dog. Then, I'd just got out of hospital when Jess developed the same problem as his mum, Sasha. So within a short space of time we had to make another decision and to have poor old Jess put to sleep – again, more tears and upset. Jess was twelve and a half when he died.

Sophie: And it was Christmas Day the next day, and Dan came up with Kerry, and cooked, and brought you Christmas dinner meals on wheels in one of Rosemary's baskets, and you had a little bit of

Christmas dinner, just a little bit. And you had your presents.

Norman: Can I just come in here. That was at the point where I got that bed sore, and that horrible nurse scrubbed it with a nail brush! I think it was because I questioned her competence over something earlier, and she obviously took the hump because, seemingly, cleaning a bed sore with a nail brush is not the appropriate treatment!

Sophie: Yes. I think the reason why you'd ended up getting a bed sore was because of the chest drain. Because of your breathing you couldn't lie down or sleep in any other position either, so all you could do was sit up in the same position. So your bottom was very sore on both sides.

So you seemed to be getting better from that surgery, but then on New Year's Day, when I was visiting you, you suddenly became acutely short of breath again, very, very, suddenly; very dramatically, in the afternoon. I was glad I was there, because you were very, very panicky again. They called the house officer to come and see you, who clearly, really didn't know what to do with you, because he kept saying to give you a saline nebuliser. They'd given you one, not saline, but Salbutamol, which is like an asthma inhaler, and it hadn't worked. And he said, "Oh, we'll give you another one."

I said, "No, you're not giving him another one. It hasn't worked. His pulse is 120. He needs a chest x-ray and a blood gas."

So I think I did your blood gas again, because he couldn't do it, and they got you a portable chest x-ray which showed that your other lung had collapsed, on the left. He got the registrar, and they put another chest drain in, which relieved that episode of shortness of breath. But you now had two chest drains: the one from the surgery, and the one they'd just had to put in because your other lung had collapsed. So that made life even more difficult really: one chest drain with fluid coming out of it, and the other draining air from the other side, so it was very difficult for you to move about or anything. They're quite wide tubes – about a centimetre, centimetre and a half across, and they came out halfway down under your arms on each side.

Norman: I pulled one out. I pulled the right-hand side one out in the shower.

Sophie: You did. It had been in for a long time, and it had become quite macerated, which means the skin had become quite wet and fragile around the chest drain, and I was helping you in the shower and you…

Norman: Caught it under the chair.

Sophie: You caught it under the chair, and managed to pull
            the right one out, and that was an emergency.

Norman: That was when we met that horrible fucking Latvian
            or whatever.

Sophie: That horrible Eastern European doctor who came
            and poked his fingers in it, without gloves on and
            without washing his hands, which we weren't very
            impressed about. Anyway, he came and he re-sited
            the chest drain, but after that, you got multi-drug-
            resistant pneumonia, then you got multi-drug-
            resistant E. coli, didn't you? Pneumonia, and…

Norman: Was that because he hadn't washed his hands?

Sophie: Well, I don't know what it was down to, but it was a
            hospital acquired infection. It could have been down
            to that. And, I suppose you gradually got better, but
            you were never really quite well. Your temperature
            and everything was always okay. And you were
            desperate, desperate to come home. You were very,
            very thin; you'd lost a lot of weight, and looking back,
            I think I should have said, why didn't they increase
            your peg feed? Because you were only getting 500
            mls of peg feed overnight, and they should have got
            the dietician to come and see you, because you were
            malnourished by the time you came out of hospital.
            But I suppose you're under so much stress at the
            time, that you can't be thinking about everything,

really. So they thought you were well enough to come home, come February. Was it February? It was, wasn't it? Yeah, February 14. And I myself wasn't...

Norman: I clearly wasn't.

Sophie: You clearly wasn't. I wasn't convinced, but I thought well, we'll give it a go...

Norman: They're the experts.

Sophie: ...we'll see what happens. So I took you home...

Chapter 14

One day, I took Scooter and the rest of the clan up to a field with a public footpath running through it. I let the dogs out of the back of the van and they would normally run straight into the field. But according to this woman, the dog came from the side of the van and bit her. I never saw it, but she and her two pals were fuckin' agitated about all this. I'm thinking, *the dog is half blind and half deaf! She must have run over his toes with her bike*! But she hotly denied that she touched him, and it was totally out of character for Scooter to bite anybody, but according to the women, he had. I gave them my name and address and told them they could do what they liked: phone the police if they wanted. That was entirely up to them. They duly did. The women phoned the police.

The policeman came to the door and was horrible. His opening gambit was: "We can either do this the easy way or the hard way. The hard way is I arrest you and the easy way is I take your details."

So, he was a prick. He showed me a photo of what Scooter had done, which was to bite the woman's arse, and she had a bruise there. I was taken into the police station because I had admitted liability, but I wasn't actually charged. However, they were going to have to take my DNA. So I have got my DNA Profile on the police database, because my dog allegedly bit a cyclist! Bit of rough justice, I thought!

About three or four years ago, my pal, Bally, died up in Perth. Bally was living with Jim's sister, Morag, and their daughter Sarah. Sarah is very clever and very successful in her dramatic arts, I believe. Bally had lymphoma, the same as me, but his attitude towards his illness was a little bit different to mine. He seemed to revel in the illness, whereas I've not really given it any time, to be honest. I felt he played the cancer card for all it was worth. Maybe if he had been a bit more positive and a bit more... I dunno... willing to help himself, he might have survived a bit longer. I don't mean that in a nasty way. It just seemed that his take on his illness was the complete opposite to mine.

Duncan arrived. He is our little west highland terrier that we got from a pub. The couple who owned him were splitting up, so we got Duncan, who has turned out to be not a bad wee dog. Good for a terrier, I think: good company and a bit of a laugh. When he was a puppy, we'd gone up to Scotland. We took Duncan to Lunan Bay on the east coast of Scotland, north of Forfar. It's a beautiful Bay. Duncan had a whale of a time, then we drove up to Stonehaven, which is a strange place. It's a bit like Aberdeen in that it doesn't matter when you go, it always seems to be freezing. They have outdoor swimming pools right on the beach and there was a strong gale, strong enough to move boulders, and it was whipping up the sand which then stings you – and that's in the height of summer!

We walked around Stonehaven for while and had a nice white pudding supper and fish and chips. Duncan was thirsty, so we went into the pet shop and bought him a wee bowl and a litre bottle of water, which he polished off. Then he had some chips and stuff, and was a happy wee dog. When we were driving home, Duncan started to squeak. We didn't think he needed the toilet as he'd done all that, but we didn't consider he was just a little dog and had just drunk a litre of water. So he climbed onto the front seat and then he climbed up Sophie's arm and braced himself between Sophie's head and the car head-rest, cocked his leg and pissed on Sophie's head. It was really quite funny.

Now, I want to talk about the walk Sophie and I did when we were up in Perth to the Glen Finnan viaduct. Now, the Glen Finnan viaduct is just a little bit further on than Lochearnhead in Perthshire. It's quite a beautiful bit of scenery and there's this old railway viaduct running along it. Sophie had always wanted to go to the viaduct and there is a footpath, which must run from Lochearnhead station up to the viaduct but we were following the signs. There was me and Soph; Jess and little Duncan (it was just before we got Max) . This was before our last great walk, really, and it's a bit sad thinking about that. Anyway, we parked the car in Lochearnhead and it was one of those days when one minute it was boiling hot, and the next minute, it was chucking it down with rain. I had jeans, boots, T-shirt and a waterproof motorcycle jacket on and Sophie had decided just to take a sweat top.

So that was it. We had the two dogs. No water, no provisions – bugger all, really. So we set off following the signs. One sign that said 'footpath' led off at right angles,

so we said "This must be it, then," and we started to climb
it. It was like the North Face of the Eiger! There was an
old river bed, only filled with water in the winter when
the snow melted and the run-off had started, so we were
both climbing over the scree and rubble. It was boiling
hot at this point and I'd got this big jacket on. I was about
buggered and my hips were killing me. So, I ditched the
jacket in this gorse hedge so that nobody could see it, and
we carried on our ascent. We got to the top, and it took
me about half an hour to recover, but the dogs loved it,
of course. We got to the old railway line and turned right
towards the viaduct, which was about four miles away.
By the time we got there, it had been sunny, raining, and
sunny again, so we were all damp and claggy. By this
time, we were also reduced to drinking from small rivulets
coming down from the hill – nice water actually – and
eating wild strawberries. I had one Satsuma in my pocket
that I shared with my wife. I may add: I was so hungry, I
could have eaten the skin! So, we had half a Satsuma each,
a handful of wild strawberries and as much water as we
wanted, really.

Well, it took forever to get to this Glenn Finnan
viaduct! We must have left Perth, I imagine, about 10
o'clock in the morning and got to Lochearnhead at around
quarter to eleven, so we probably didn't start walking the
railway track till about mid-day. It had taken us about
three hours to get from there to the viaduct and I was
completely bollocked; my hips were absolutely killing
me. We were going out with Jim that evening and this
was now 3 o'clock in the afternoon! We had to make

tracks back as soon as we arrived, and we went down the same scree so I could retrieve my jacket. It took us five hours to get back to the car! We had to call Jim and Theresa and tell them what the crack was. I thought at one point I was going to have to call out the mountain rescue, I was so knackered. However, I persevered as I'd rather have crawled out on my hands and knees than have the embarrassment of that spread across the Perthshire Advertiser and the Dundee Courier! However, it was beautiful. I loved it and I'm glad I was able to do it, and to do it with Soph and the dogs. It's just a bit sad that I can't do that sort of thing anymore. I'm gutted that I can't.

Norman: Want to talk about when we went to Newcastle for the lung transplant operation. So I'd been to see Dr Steiner regarding my chest and what not, and he basically said that I had end-stage lung disease.

Sophie: End stage respiratory failure; yes.

Norman: Yeah, well, sorry – end stage respiratory failure. And I had asked him about a transplant, a lung transplant, so he said he would refer me to Newcastle. The choice was between Oxford or Newcastle, but well, it was north and half the journey for my family if anything ever came off. It would have been a bit easier. So off we went to Newcastle for the assessment. Over to you.

Sophie: Just trying to think back now. This was relatively

recently, wasn't it? But what year was it?

Norman: It was 2009.

Sophie: 2009. So you had to go up once at the beginning
            of the year, I think it may have been February,
            something like that.

Norman: March time we would have gone.

Sophie: Yeah, so in the spring we went to Newcastle, and it
            was a sort of two night job, wasn't it?

Norman: What was the name of the hotel, the hospital?

Sophie: Jessop... It was in Jesmond.

Norman: Yeah, but what was the name of the hospital? Sorry.

Sophie: Freeman. Freeman Hospital.

Norman: Yeah, the hotel was the Rosemount.

Sophie: And the hotel was the Rosemount.

Norman: I'll never forget that.

Sophie: Oh God, yeah. So yes, went to the Freeman Hospital,
            and it was a three day, two night assessment, and
            remember – I'd got a lecture I still hadn't finished,

so I spent most of the time on my laptop trying to prepare the lecture for the gynae-oncology away-day I'd been invited to lecture at. So in between you going off and doing your various bits and pieces, I sat at my laptop and worked out my lecture. But that's a side issue.

So we went up, and they spent a lot of time imparting information about what a transplant would involve. There was a lot of assessment to determine whether or not you were physically up to it. Mentally and socially up to it, as well: whether you had got the right social set-up, and the right attitude to be able to cope with having a solid organ transplant. And there were lots of facts and figures, weren't there? About how well people do, and survival rates. So we spent a lot of time talking to the transplant nurses; had to spend some time talking to a social worker about social set-up, and things like that. And you had to have lots of tests.

Norman: What is a social set-up?

Sophie: Well, just who you've got living with you at home, where you live, what support you've got, what financial support you've got – that kind of thing.

Norman: Right.

Sophie: Because the organs are precious, I suppose. They don't want to give them away to people that are not going to manage to take their pills, their anti-rejection medicine.

Norman: Or go boozing or smoking.

Sophie: Or go boozing or smoking or whatever. Yeah, so we spent a lot of time talking, and then you had to have your lung function test, blood tests, and your echocardiogram done. You had to have a walking test with the physios, didn't you, to see what your sats and things were like. What other tests did you have?

Norman: Lung function. Liver…

Sophie: Infection screening.

Norman: Got all my bloods done.

Sophie: So that took a day or so, to go through all that process, and imparting the information and things. And then they have a meeting at the end of the week, don't they, and they decide whether you're a yes or a no or a maybe.

Norman: Is that the second visit?

Sophie: No, the first visit. So on the first visit, the upshot was that they thought you were too well at that time –

which makes you laugh, really – to have a transplant.
They thought that over all, your lung function
wasn't quite bad enough to warrant the risk of going
through a transplant. They'd got some reservations
about whether you were fit enough to have it done,
too, but they didn't say no at that stage. What they
said was that they'd like to see you back again in six
months. And did you see the chap that had had the
transplant, the first time or the second time?

Norman: Well, tell me about your hospital overnight stay and
accommodation in Newcastle.

Sophie: Oh in Newcastle. Well, the first time we went to
Newcastle, we stayed in a hotel called Rosemount,
which was cheap.

Norman: It looked lovely from the outside.

Sophie: But it wasn't very cheerful. And they'd overcharged
us.

Norman: And there was nobody…

Sophie: And there was never any staff.

Norman: There was nobody on reception, and a lot of others
there were waiting.

Sophie: There's no reception. Yeah. And it was just not

nice. So the second time we went, I think we'd decided because it was just one night you would stay in the hospital, and I would stay in the family accommodation that they provided. Well, the accommodation for relatives was shared, and I thought, 'Oh, that's fine, it's only one night in a shared room with somebody. It doesn't matter.'

Anyway, so I went into the room, and you had to share a key with this person as well. You didn't have your own key – the usual NHS thing. But this woman I was sharing with was American, and was probably about 30 stone. She got into her nightdress, which could have doubled as a wedding marquee – this huge, white, billowing cotton thing. And as she turned the lights out, she said, "Oh, I hope you don't mind but I snore."

And she wasn't wrong. Not only did she snore, but the whole room was shaking, and I just could not sleep. I was so tired from the drive up to Newcastle and everything that had happened during the day, I needed to get to sleep but I just couldn't. So what I did was, I took my duvet and my pillows, and I went into the store cupboard and I found another duvet, and I went and I slept on a duvet on the kitchen floor, with the two doors between us shut, because it was the only way I could get any sleep. Fortunately, I'm quite used to sleeping on NHS floors, so it wasn't too much of a problem, but I did get some quite

funny looks from the other people as they were
coming into the kitchen to make their tea in the
morning.

Norman: Did the fat woman have anything to say about it?

Sophie: Well, she was terribly apologetic, but what else can
you do? So that was that. Yeah.

So the upshot of the second visit was that they
thought there was a very high chance that the blood
loss would put you into renal failure – kidney failure
– and that was just a complication that they weren't
prepared to accept. So I think it was a reasonable
decision on their part, and a reasonable decision
on your part, really. After they'd told you that they
weren't prepared to offer it to you, you said you'd
thought about it and you didn't want it anyway.
So I think everybody felt that you'd explored the
option very thoroughly, and you'd been assessed very
thoroughly, but it was a chapter that was closed. So
you parted friends.

And on the way back from that visit, that second
visit to Newcastle, you were quite ill, weren't you?

Norman: Yeah.

Sophie: You… we'd had McDonalds, we'd had some chips
and stuff in the car on the way down, and you

suddenly started to get very, very severe colicky
upper abdominal pain. You started to be sick, and
you really were not well at all. You were vomiting into
a McDonalds cup, in absolute writhing agony. And
again, it was one of those situations where you think
to yourself, right...

Norman: We were on the motorway at this point.

Sophie: ...we're on the motorway, he's being sick in a cup,
we're halfway between Newcastle and Leicester –
what do I do? What do I do? So I just managed to
drive home, just managed to get home in time for
the GP surgery closing. So with about...

Norman: You had given me morphine as soon as we got in.

Sophie: Had I given you morphine? Yes, that's right. Given
you some Oramorph as soon as we got in, and
you started to feel a bit better. I managed to ring
the GP surgery at about three minutes to six, and
fortunately, the GP was still there, and obviously,
he knows us very well. And I said, "I think Norman's
got biliary colic," which is the pain you get from
gallstones, because the symptoms that you were
having were typical of that. I said, "Can I bring him
up? Will you have a look at him? We've just got back
from Newcastle." And lovely Dr Gaunt – he was so
lovely – said, "Yeah, of course! Bring him straight
away and I'll have a look at him."

So he took you straight in, didn't he? Had a look at you up on the couch. He said, "Yeah, I think you're right. I think he's got a gallstone or biliary colic."

I said, "What should we do? Should we stay at home? Should we go into hospital?"

He said, "Look, I don't think there's any point you going into hospital, because they're not going to do anything."

So he gave me some Pethidine injections and some Cyclizine, which is an anti-sickness injection, and we went home. And he arranged a scan for you, didn't he, for gallstones, to be done as an outpatient.

Norman: That was another fun experience.

Sophie: And so you came home, and you were a little bit better, weren't you, overnight. You'd had a couple of injections and it all settled down really, as quickly as it came on. That was another experience.

Norman: Well, if you remember, you dropped me off for the scan, and you had disappeared, and this nurse had said, "Who was that, that brought you in? Was it your daughter?"

To which, of course, I was really angry, upset and annoyed that anybody could think that I was 20

years older than Sophie! For God's sake! I must
have looked like shit! Anyway, I remember after the
tests were done, I was told that I didn't have any
gallstones. And I said, "Well, I must have passed it
then."

And she said, "Well, I don't know about that, because
you would have been in terrible pain if you'd passed
it."

And I says, "Well, I was in terrible fucking pain! That's
why I'm here!"

I remember that. I remember that quite clearly.
Anyway, have you anything to add?

Sophie: Not really. So that was Newcastle.

Norman: Well, certainly because it's just a… nut house. Any
             other health problems you can remember?

Sophie: Let's just turn it off and have a think.

I began to feel a bit better by the summer of 2009 and
although I had never had any interest in gardening I felt
that I wanted to try to do something with my time. I
already had one greenhouse in the garden and I acquired
another one from Daniel, Sophie's brother. So I put the
second greenhouse up and did my beds, and that proved to
be successful.

Must tell you a funny story. I'd read an article in the female section in the paper, how when it comes to moisturising, that a woman's cleavage and breasts are the most neglected areas. You know, I just can't fathom that, because any woman's boyfriend, partner, or husband would do it! Just give them a tub of Pond's and they would just jump at the chance to put moisturising cream onto your breasts! So, you know, I was quite surprised that they'd even said that, because it just can't be right! You'll ask your man to put up shelves, so I'm sure if you asked him to put a few dollops of moisturiser on your boobs, he'd be more than happy!

There we are. That's my wee story out of the way.

Norman: Second time.

Sophie: Yeah. So six months went on, and we had to go back in September for another assessment, so off we duly did. And it was the same procedure again, really, wasn't it? Exactly the same procedure, the tests were repeated, and they compared what you'd been like six months before.

Norman: And I was actually quite well at that point. We'd been on holiday, met Joyce and Ian and whatnot. I was up and down the beach on the Segway; Joyce was falling off, and Ian was rubbish on the Segway; so yeah, everybody had a good time I think, that holiday. Anyway.

Sophie: Yeah. So it was the second time we went up, I think
            they'd assessed you. I can't really remember whether
            there was that much change in your lung function,
            I think it had gone down a bit, but you were pretty
            stable, like you say, in terms of what you could do; in
            terms of function.

Norman: And I asked if I could see someone who had just had
            a transplant. So I spoke to Ray, and it was apparent
            to me that he was so much worse than I was prior
            to this transplant, and he was… He had reached the
            point where he was having people bath him and
            wash him, which I was able to do and still am, so he
            was…

Sophie: And he was stuck on his chair, wasn't he? He couldn't
            walk around at all.

Norman: No. So I'd been doing my own research into
            transplants, and the number of people that are dead
            after five years was half, I think. The average life span
            was five years post-transplant. I'd have to look at the
            figures again, but you know, to go through all that for
            an extra five years! I thought, 'I've probably got five
            years without it, to be honest!' So I'd made up my
            mind that the transplant was probably not a route I
            would go down.

Sophie: Yes, I think you'd already decided, because the
            surgery itself is gruelling, to say the least. And then

you'd have to spend several weeks, 12 weeks or
something, after the surgery, living in a flat up there.

Norman: Three months.

Sophie: It was months, living in a flat up there, whilst you
            were kept an eye on and assessed.

Norman: In a hospital flat.

Sophie: In a hospital flat, not anywhere nice. No, I don't think
            it would have been, given that I had to sleep on the
            floor in the kitchen that night, because that woman
            was snoring so loudly. So you had decided that it
            wasn't for you, and I think that was the right decision.

Norman: We decided together.

Sophie: We talked about it and decided that actually, no,
            you'd had enough. You'd been through enough, and
            you'd had enough, and you weren't prepared to go
            through that.

Norman: Because it seemed to me, the benefits didn't
            outweigh the procedure.

Sophie: No, that's right. The procedure itself was just too
            gruelling, after everything you'd been though. They'd
            also looked at things again, and basically decided
            that you weren't suitable for transplant, because

your lungs had both been stuck down before, so
that would involve surgical complexity, and probably
involve quite a large blood loss during surgery. And
because your kidney function is just teetering on the
brink of acceptability.

Norman: Is it still?

When I was first admitted into the Glenfield Hospital
with my lung problems, my sister Joyce had come down
to visit. At the time, I remember telling Joyce that I was
concerned about Sophie's health and how she was coping,
emotionally, with my ongoing ill health. I spoke to
Sophie, too, trying to make sure she was ok and suggested
she speak to someone about what she was having to cope
with. Sophie was quite adamant that she didn't need to
speak to anyone, and now, three and a half years later, we
find that things are very difficult between us. Sophie has
now agreed to go for counselling at Loros and says she
finds it very helpful. I know she thinks that I didn't really
care about her and how she was coping, but I did. I also
find the counselling at Loros helpful.

I just wonder if there could have been any alternative
way to get my lungs back up, rather than gluing them
in place. Because ultimately, that is what stopped me
from getting any further treatment or a lung transplant.
I wonder if the job was a quick fix or a cheap option over
anything else.

This is April 2010 I'm going to talk about now. I'd just
started learning the guitar. Whilst I was recovering, we

decided to go away on holiday to Wells-Next-the-Sea. We'd been before and we loved the place. We had also enjoyed staying in our little caravan. I wasn't able to do much, but Sophie set it all up nicely. We'd no sooner got the caravan set up when it started to piss with rain. I'd made all the arrangements for my oxygen to be delivered to the campsite so that I'd have all I needed for getting out and about. We were supposed to be away for ten days, but Sophie was on the Segway on the beach, speeding along, when she hit a load of ruts in the sand and was spat off the Segway. She badly twisted her knee, so that was one disaster. Of course, I was in the electric wheelchair. The weather was shite. It was pissing with rain every day, and was cold and miserable. It rained for five solid days – and on day five we just looked at each other and said, "Well, it's not raining now, but since we were surrounded by black clouds, shall we just pack up and go now before the rain starts again?"

I did what I could to pack, rolling leads up and things, and Sophie made several dashes backwards and forwards, packing the car. We managed to finish the job before the rain came, and set off home. We had Duncan dog with us. Rosie and Jeff, our very helpful neighbours, were looking after our dog Scooter because he was too old to travel, and Max, of course.

When we got back to our house, we realised very quickly that Scooter was quite unwell with a chest infection, so we took him to the vet. The vet examined Scooter and said that he was in respiratory failure and, basically, there wasn't really a great deal they could do for him. I didn't try with antibiotics, since the poor old dog was tired and done; the vet said he was going to die and the kindest thing we could do was to put him to sleep before he got short of breath. I didn't miss the irony with my own situation! So Scooter was put to sleep, which meant I'd lost my three dogs in five months, which was very, very sad. I'd lost my pals, really. It broke my heart to see Scooter put to sleep, since I had a real soft spot for that dog because he was a bit wilful and only ever did what he could get away with. He wouldn't volunteer to chase a ball or go for a swim; he was quite happy just lying in his bed – usually on the couch, that meant! It wasn't a good month – that was Scooter's demise.

I think with the way I was feeling about my own health situation, with it never getting any better; it was around this time that I sank into a kind of depression. We also decided at this juncture to sell our caravan as I wasn't able to help with it much and the five days of solid rain had kind of put us off caravanning for life.

We still have Duncan, the little terrier, and Max the new Shepherd. Just prior to my collapsed lungs we bought Max a backpack to try to get him to use up his energy by carrying things we got from the market. This back pack was lovely and well made. We took him to the market once and we got our fruit and vegetables and loaded Max up. He loved it and everyone thought it was a great idea that Max was actually doing a bit of work. It's a shame we can't get out and about, as he could be carrying the water bottles for me. Picnics would have been good, too. Max would have loved that.

Unfortunately, about a month later I was in hospital, buggered.

When I was first admitted to The Glenfield Hospital with my lung problem, Rosie and Jeff, our neighbours, had spotted Sophie walking all these dogs on her own and noticed I hadn't been around for a while. It was around Christmas time and Rosie felt compelled to call in on Sophie to see if she could be of any help with the dogs. Rosie was convinced that Sophie's man had probably left her for some other woman, just before Christmas! So Sophie invited this crazy old woman into our house and we've been friends with them ever since. Rosie's husband Jeff looked after the dogs while Sophie was at work and I was in hospital, and he still continues to look after our German Shepherd, Max, since I am no longer able to walk our dogs. Rosie cooks us many, many meals and generally looks after us. Rosie and Jeff are extremely kind to us and very generous in giving of their time and company, cooking for us and walking Max, while letting me do the crosswords in the daily paper! I can't praise them enough. I don't know how we would manage without them. In fact, it would be fair to say we couldn't manage without them. We love them to bits. They have both been absolutely brilliant to us.

I started gardening when I was well enough. I grow a lot of different fruit and vegetables and I feel I've got quite a good little home industry going with my chutney and jam making. My products are much appreciated by my family and friends who reap the benefits of my hard work!

I've tried other new ventures to keep me amused. For

example, I play the guitar. I had lessons from a bloke, Bill, who was a brilliant guitarist. He could listen to something on the radio or stereo, and after a few minutes he could play it back, note for note, but his lessons were never structured in a way that suited my learning. I was beginning to cool off from his lessons, and at the same time I was going back into hospital and said I'd ring Bill when I got out, but I never did. After a couple of months, I picked up the guitar again and I strum away to myself.

I do a lot more reading nowadays and am happy to read a variety of books. I began watching a bit of TV again. We were without a TV for a while, through choice, but Jeff gave me a present of a TV on my last return from hospital, which was really kind of him. He also got the box and set the whole thing up for us. Of course, I'm still waiting on him giving me the money back for the licensing fee! Only joking, Jeff! It was a really nice surprise for me. Thank you, Jeff.

For a while, I had my trike project on the go and my friend Gaz has been a good help with that. We have made a lot of changes to the bike to make it suitable for me to handle and use.

We also have a number of different people who come around our house each week. We pay to get some domestic help and our cleaner, "Tracy love", and her daughter, Nicola, keep the house straight. We've also got someone who does our ironing, which is a good help, and a hardworking friend of Rosie and Jeff comes and does a bit of gardening. Sophie works very hard at her full time job as a doctor, so it means if we have all the domestic jobs out of the way, she doesn't have to do so much when she comes home. While I do what I can, it isn't a lot, and therefore it's necessary to have outside help.

There has also been an increase of medical staff who come to the house quite often now, particularly if I need antibiotics administered intravenously.

Chapter 15

I've gained a wonderful wife and from that, I've got more than I expected. I never expected to marry someone who would be doctor. It's good to have someone on your side. I don't think the person needs to be medically qualified but as long as they have a brain in their head and they are willing to ask awkward questions, they are an asset. Otherwise, you get nowhere.

Apart from the fact that I'm now unable to do very much, and I've sometimes asked the question, "why me?" and felt angry; I think, all things considered, that I've been pretty content really. I've got a few friends I can trust and I'm happy with those two or three friends. I don't need acquaintances. I've got a great sister who is very supportive.

I don't think my wife and I have ever had a serious argument. We fall out, but we always make up. Well, pretty much, apart from during the last two years, when I've been sinking into deep pits of depression and I've been silent for days – not Sophie. Prior to this point, we've always made up by night time. Outside, I'm silent, but inside I'm crying out for someone to put their arms around me and give me a hug. But I can't ask for it and they think I don't want a hug, because I'm being silent, but that's not the case. The trouble is, it's not enough to get a hug once, because I'll say, "Piss off". I need the person (that is, Sophie) to keep doing it until the time comes that I'll accept it. But of course, how many times is Sophie going to suffer rejection before she says "Well, bugger you then! Come out of it on your own, in your own time!"? If Sophie is feeling angry too, then my silence feeds her anger.

This Christmas past, I was very depressed. However, I'm now on "sunshine" pills, as I call them, and they keep a smile on my face. The tablets help, to be honest, but the trouble is, I don't like taking pills. But if I don't take the "sunshine" pills, then I slowly sink back until I'm depressed again. I made a judgement to come off my pills once, which didn't help really, so, I won't be doing that again. I'll let the Doctor decide when I should come off the anti-depressants.

It might seem, over all this time, that I'm handing more control over to the Doctors in relation to my care, but I don't think that is so, as I've never really gone against the Doctors' advice very often. I've always had good advice from Doctors but I now realise that what they actually do is a series of educated guesses. I don't think they really know entirely what to do with me! I've been ill for so long that sometimes I make my own series of educated guesses which don't always quite tie up with the Doctors' guesses! For instance, if the Doctor wants to reduce my steroids from time to time, they will say, "Take this amount off the dosage every day," while I'll think that's too much. So I'll cut it down by the amount *I* think is right. When I go back a month later, the Doctor will ask how I'm getting on.

I'll say, "I never cut it down to the level that you said, and I feel I'm ok. So I will continue as I am doing."

And the Doctor usually responds by saying, "Well, if you're feeling fine, it's your body, just continue the way you are."

The Doctors now know that I'm my own person and I will tell them if I'm unhappy with their thoughts. I've reduced the steroids in the past as they have suggested, and have felt very unwell because of the reduction, so they now know that I'm not prepared to go through that again. If the Doctors give me good advice I'll take it, but if I don't think it's good, then I won't take it and I think they know this. I never really tweak what I call the "big hitters", that's the immuno-suppressants or anything like that, because I really don't know enough about them. The use of painkillers and similar drugs is really up to me. The Doctors leave that up to me as long as I don't go over the prescribed daily dose. I've learned quite a lot about pills and their effects.

As a patient, I don't want to be in hospital, but some of these horrible nurses behave as though they don't want to be there either. The least they could do is put a smile on their faces. We can all have bad days at work, but don't take it out on the patients because it's not the patients' fault. The nurse chose the job – I didn't choose to be here, ill. The fact that there are ill people at all gives the medical person a job, so we are, in fact, their clients. I hate going into hospital. Although I have been given sleeping pills, I can't sleep there. It is so noisy. I also have no appetite when I'm in hospital and I don't enjoy hospital food. This then creates problems for me regarding weight loss.

The doctors know that I don't want to be in hospital

unless it is absolutely necessary and because my wife is a doctor, they will send me home and give my wife my drugs to administer to me. These are drugs that are not readily available in the community and only for use in the hospital. In addition, the District Nurses will come round and do my injections if my wife is at work. This is much better, because I get nice food, I have a comfortable bed, and I don't have people moaning, groaning, screeching or giving me germs. I've had hospital-contracted infections and they're not nice. Also, you go into a hospital ward and everybody wants to know what's wrong with you. I feel it's no one's business why I'm in hospital, and I don't want to know why they're in there. I just want to be left alone to get better, and be out as quickly as possible. The last time I was in hospital was Jan 2011. I was in a side ward because I had flu, and that was OK. I like my own company. I'd rather be on my own than in the company of fools. I'm pretty much self-reliant and don't need or get a lot of support from the nurses. If I can't do what's required, like have a bath or a shower, I wait for Sophie to come in to help me.

I don't know what it is like to be in hospital to need that high level of care, but if I did need it and I had no partner and no chance of improvement, I think I would top myself. It's awfully sad to see these poor souls who are dribbling mince down their chins. It is also very off-putting. If it was a horse or a dog, you would humanely put them to sleep and I can't see why they think human beings should be made to suffer. I'd rather have all the drips and things removed from me and just be allowed to go. I've let my wishes be known to Sophie and said that if I lose all control of my faculties, and start soiling myself, don't even bother – just stick a pillow over my face.

To be honest, I've thought of suicide in the past and I have had enough morphine to do that. I have thought about it, but only in the same way as I think about a lot of things – it's an option, but not a route I'm willing to go down. I don't have the courage to do it, for all its badness, and the amount of times I've sat at home or have been in hospital terribly ill, in a lot of pain and thought, "I wish I was dead!" Then when I get better, I think, "Well, I'm glad I'm not dead!" I can understand where people are at, when they think "enough's enough." I'm not really in too much pain. I do have terrible arthritis, for which I take medication, but it's all controllable, so I'm not in real, physical discomfort unless I exert myself.

The transition from being the angry person that I was to the calmer more accepting person that I am now came gradually. I didn't wake up one day and decide – that came later (because I had an epiphany, but that was much, much later). The actual going from being angry and bitter to calmer and more accepting was gradual and probably peaked when I was going to attack my wife when I was about 31 years old. After all my karate training, you'd think I'd see that coming, eh? Blind fury! That was the climax, and then came a plateau. I got married at 29, so it was probably in the second year of my marriage, when the climax and plateau occurred. Although I still ask, "why me?" I have a handle on my anger now. Although this has all happened, I recognise that it's not worth losing my wife, my house, my job.

Although I think since the time that my lungs collapsed, I've become angrier and angrier again. I'm so frustrated by my immobility and just watching people walk, run, cycle… and couples hand in hand; I think – "me and poor Sophie can't do that!" I feel very odd. I'm only 48; Sophie is 39 and has a husband like me! I feel heartily sorry for us both, that life has come to this. That's where my frustration stems from. I've never been one for sitting back and accepting my fate. I've always tried to improve my odds, by being proactive, going to the gym, eating properly, growing stuff in the garden, making chutneys and so on; but with this condition, I know that there is nothing I can do to improve my lungs and the condition is just going to continue to get worse. And it's soul-destroying. I cannot begin to tell you just how sad it is to know that you're dying and can't do a bloody thing about it! It's like waiting for the lights to go out. I'm not used to not having a chance, and so I take it out on everybody else. That is why I'm a miserable bastard a lot of the time.

But considering the fact that they only gave me a matter of a few years – and that was over 25 years ago – well, I'm a statistical anomaly! A blip on the chart! My wife says I'm a "statistical outlier"! And my consultant, the last time I saw her, welcomed me in with, "Here's Mr Will, my patient, with more lives than a cat!" That's the first time she's ever cracked a joke! It's the first time I've heard her, anyway – it's taken her a long time for the barrier to have been broken down between me and Dr.

Hunter. She's always kept a very distinct doctor-patient relationship, whereas a lot of the other doctors are quite chummy. She isn't. I met someone up in Rotherham at the hospital who was having the same treatment as me who was also being treated by Dr Hunter in Leicester. He was asking who was in charge of me, to which I replied, "Dr Hunter". He had been seeing her for a year and a half and his reply was, "Oh, not that old witch!"

I've been seeing Dr. Hunter for over 14 years now. I like her and she is very knowledgeable. Frankly, she can be as much of an old witch as she likes, as long as she does her job properly. I don't think she has the same rapport with many of her patients as I have with her. Our relationship over the years has only chilled out a little bit, maybe, in the last eighteen months. I don't think it's because she is concerned about emotional attachment to patients who are going through the mill. I think she wants her patients to recognise that she isn't someone who is easily distracted. I think she obviously takes her role seriously and she wants everyone else to take her position seriously, too. She's the 'head' one.

Given my situation and me being a bit of a phenomenon, if I get referred anywhere by Dr Hunter, I rarely, rarely ever see anyone who isn't a Consultant. I'm usually seen by Seniors; not because they know me, but when Dr Hunter writes to them, I think she gives them an outline of what I've been through. I think she makes it clear that she wants me to be seen by "them", that is: the best. She will write to the Head of Department or Chief Consultant directly and request that he or she sees me.

Going back to my anger and managing my attitude, I think I've kind of lost a bit of that now. My tank of mental energy is getting really depleted and I'm tired of fighting it; but if I stop fighting it I don't know what will happen. Even if I do stop fighting it, the outcome's not going to change. I'm not passively accepting it, and it's not that I don't really care – it's just that whatever I do, it's not going to improve my situation. When I had cancer and was fighting it, I felt that there was a light at the end of the tunnel. Even although I accepted that there was going to be a rocky road ahead; ultimately, I believed that beating the cancer was achievable. What I've got now is incurable, and I know that. It's just going to get worse and I can't do a great deal about it. I feel disempowered because I feel like I'm completely at the mercy of the illness and the only people that can do much about it are doctors. I really can't contribute. When I was fighting cancer and doing my training, I felt I was doing my bit to keep myself fit, but now I can't train because I've got no puff. I just don't feel I've got any control over my life and that's been my target – the outcome of so many years, when I was making sure I did have some control over my life. Every time the doctors said that I had liver failure and kidney failure, there was always hope. But now, to be honest, the only thing I can hope for is for some fantastic new stem cell treatment. They have now begun making lung tissue from stem cells, but they reckon it will be fifteen years before it is ready for clinical trial and I don't know if I'm going to make fifteen years. Sometimes I think I will, and sometimes I think I won't make fifteen minutes.

I've written here, "I don't know if I know if I'm feeling well because I am actually feeling well, or if I'm just used to feeling different levels of crap. Is my feeling well actually normal? Is it a poorly person's normal, or is it a normal person's poorly?"

What I'm trying to say is, it's been so long since I felt well that when I actually feel well, I don't know if it's what a normal person would feel – or is it just a lighter level of crap? I don't know. Some days I do feel reasonably ok, and a lot of days I feel a little bit below par. To be fair, there are very few days when I would have no grumbles, especially now with this breathing thing. It's so frustrating, more than anything else. It's not particularly painful and it's only distressing when I do too much. Then I get out of breath and I feel like I'm suffocating, which is horrible. It's been so long since I've been classed as physically well that I can't really remember how it feels. That's a bit sad, really. I think, healthwise, I've just got various levels of crapness. Some days it's light crap and some days it's really bad crap. That's about as much as I can say on that.

Since I bought the trike two years ago, physically, I have deteriorated. It's a big old trike. It's a Triumph Rocket III motorcycle trike, which to the uninitiated, is huge. It's the biggest motorcycle in the world, or was at the time. It has a 2.3 litre engine in it. It's pretty massive and takes a lot of muscle to do any great distance on it. I can manage about an hour at a time if I'm lucky, on a reasonably straight road. It's when you steer it round the corners that you feel the weight of it. I'd like to go to the

Eden Project, but I don't think I'll be going on the trike, to be honest. You dream the dream and that sustains you and keeps you going for a while. You try to make things work for you and try to think out of the box for other ideas on how to enjoy a hobby, but maybe the Triumph Rocket was too big a bike, and in reality we should have gone for something smaller.

I don't think I'm afraid of death, but the manner in which I might die scares me more. I don't want to be lying choking in my own pleural fluids, for instance, and that's what scares me most. I'll be drugged up to the eyeballs and slowly just waiting. I think my picture of cancer patients is of them losing weight, and dying slowly over months and months – I don't want that. That's my biggest fear. I deal with these thoughts because if I was told that I had x number of months, and it got to the point where it was too painful, or I couldn't go to the toilet on time, I know in the past I have had the means to take my own life, but now I don't have enough morphine to do this. Just now, I'm in limbo because the days just merge into one another. I don't plan anything – like a holiday or anything, because I don't know if I'm going to be well on that particular day. So my wife and I don't make any plans, which means it doesn't give you anything to look forward to.

Making a plan for something like the cinema isn't a problem, but if I wanted to book a holiday in advance I can't do that because I don't want to be shelling out thousands of pounds on a holiday and then find I'm too ill to go. I suppose I could budget for a deposit lost, and then I wouldn't be so surprised or disappointed if I had to cancel. If that was the condition I booked the holiday under, I suppose that would be alright. The fact that I might lose money is a problem for me! I'm also conscious of letting other people down, like, if my wife gets all excited, and then I can't go I would feel guilty, although Sophie is good at understanding the situation.

I was worried in case I wasn't well enough to go back to Edinburgh with Joyce and Ian after them coming down to collect me. I do still get enthusiastic about things and I'm enjoying the idea that something is being done about writing a book. I'm upbeat again. Something different is happening, and it's a challenge and perhaps because of this I can get up, and Joyce can get down a bit more often.

So there's that. I kind of live in the here and now. I think it's the only way to deal with it. After my lungs collapsed and I got out of hospital, I was very frustrated but I learned to live with the pace my body could go at. I don't expect too much and I try not to think about what I could do if I wasn't ill, because it's pointless and unproductive.

I just kind of wake up in the morning, edge my way into the day and see how I feel. If it's nice weather, I go into the garden, or if it's pouring with rain, I'll read or practise on the guitar. Going back to when it was cancer, I felt I had something to fight against, but now that my illness isn't beatable, I feel rudderless. No light to guide me. I always had a light at the end of the tunnel, but now I feel that the light is extinguished. I suffered a real bout of depression last Christmas, 2010. There are no highs and no lows in my life – it's very even. I can't factor highs in, because I can't plan. Even to plan for the next day is difficult. I said to Joyce, "I will know tonight if I feel able enough to visit Noreen (my sister), tomorrow." Not only because I may not feel physically able but also because of my mental state. I will just say, "I can't be bothered," because that's what I feel. I'm not out of the woods as far as the depression goes – it's still there. I'm on tablets and they are helping, but I'm still struggling to get motivated. It's not particular to dying or getting ill, I don't think. It's just there.

During the past twenty years I've had some positive things come out of this negative situation. Two years ago, before my lungs collapsed, whilst my chest was a bit dodgy, there was a lot of good stuff that came out of it. I felt that I was a better person than I had been, because I could understand others more, having been through so much myself. If I saw someone struggling, I would help them; whereas before, while I certainly wouldn't have walked past anyone if they needed help previously, I may not have even noticed. In the past, before being ill, I used to drink quite a lot, but I stopped all that after diagnosis and I trained more, to try to increase my fitness level.

I suppose one of the things about chronic long term illness is loneliness, really, because obviously I'm unable to work so I just don't get any real social interaction. People who used to come round to see me don't come so often. I know that people have got their own lives, but I just don't think many people we know really appreciate how bad things are. People who say that they are going to help and then forget, can they just stop fucking offering? That would be good, because I kind of get my hopes up that somebody will turn up and do a couple of wee jobs, or keep me company, or walk a dog. There have been a few times when I've been let down – but enough said, really.

The people you think won't, let you down, and the people you think of as acquaintances show you kindness you wouldn't believe! For example, I had an old boy, John, who did odd building jobs, recommended to me by Jeff, and I asked him to sort out the patio and a bit of repointing required on the garden wall. He heard of my plight, and he often drops by for a couple of hours, has a coffee and a chat and brings me his old motor cycle magazines that he's finished with. He's offered to take me out to Mallory Park if I want to go when he goes. He's seventy and as fit as a flea, a bit like Jeff in that respect. I do envy these old boys! I knew him from nowhere, and he's done a lot to cheer me up. He's of the same mould as Rosie and Jeff. Yet people I've known for years and try to keep in touch with never get back to me. Illness is a real leveller!

In 2010, I went up to Perth to do the electrics in Jim's mum and dad's kitchen. Well, actually, I advised Jim where to put all the electrics, and he did the donkey work. Then I did all the connections for them, which saved his folks a few quid. It felt good doing something for them as they have always been good to me.

I remember Jim's pal, the Virgin Marti, taking the piss out of me, calling me Jacques Cousteau, because I was breathing through my oxygen tank on my back. I actually felt quite hurt by that, because I wasn't well, and taking the piss out of someone unwell… he'd just pushed it too far – the pair of them had.

A funny story I heard.

First off, I was up for my treatment in Rotherham this week and the guy on the machine next to me said he'd done a really embarrassing thing. What he'd done was, he'd been in a garden centre and had stopped off in the cafe for a coffee, and at the opposite table there was a woman with a little baby. He was basically staring at it and then he walked over and said to the lady, "What a lovely baby!" and proceeded to coochie-coo at it. Then he suddenly realised that the woman was breast-feeding the baby. I pissed myself. I thought that was really funny.

Chapter 16

2011 hadn't been a good year for me. It had been a long
winter and I hadn't been able to do very much, so by
the time summer came round, I was quite weak. With
hindsight I should have been doing some exercise on the
exercise bike and lifting the 2.5 and 5kg weights I have.
By summer, I was just so crap. Worse than normal crap,
even. The infections started, of course, and they always get
me down, so summer wasn't brilliant.

As we moved onto autumn, I was becoming more and
more depressed. I'd sunk way below what was even bad
for me. I'd had enough. My wife was busy at work and
was stressed out there, and I was fuckin' miserable, so she
would be miserable back to me. We weren't getting on.
Also, I seemed to be getting a sinus infection, which got
much worse after visiting Sophie's mum's, and I had all
this snot coming down the back of my throat. That was
October or November time. I just felt miserable. During
the journey back, Sophie and I had a mini-argument about
traffic and road positioning. Turned out I was right, but
you can't tell Sophie that she's wrong. After the argument,
I felt totally fed-up and done with the world. At home,
we still didn't speak and as I'd had enough of everything,
I decided I was going to end my life. However, I actually
think it's wrong to end your life, so I was in a quandary,
and I'm also a bit of a coward. Knowing my luck, I'd take
an overdose of tablets and make my liver function worse,

but I'd still be alive. Slitting my wrists would be difficult, as I'm not a fan of blood and I wouldn't like to leave a mess for anyone to clear up. Basically, I'm just a coward. What I decided to do was to stop taking my feeds, which were taken directly into my stomach, and to stop my medication. I would only drink water to stop me feeling that my mouth was full of wallpaper paste. Yeah, I decided to withdraw everything, and the hope was that I wouldn't have to prolong it, because my heart would give out or I'd go into some kind of organ failure, and basically that would do it for me.

So I started my regime and got to day five. Sophie wasn't speaking to me, so she wasn't giving a fuck, at that point. She didn't look in on me and when she came home from work, she just left me to it, which was fine by me. I got up daily for a glass of water and that did me, all day. On day five, I realised that I had to go to the hospital for an appointment because if I don't pitch up, they phone me at home to find out what is wrong. I thought, "I'll pre-empt all that and keep my appointment, get the stuff done, get back home and the hospital staff won't be any the wiser of my regime."

By day five, I'd easily gone past the one hundred hours of no food, no medication and little water, and I felt terrible. Worse, by the time I got to the hospital. On arrival, the nurse was trying to take blood from me, but she couldn't find a vein as I was so dehydrated. The staff said, "There's something wrong here," and asked me what was going on. I told them my tale. They arranged immediately for me to go to the Psychiatric Unit at the

Glenfield Hospital, and I realised it was for my own good so I went voluntarily. I didn't have to be sectioned.

Some people may think that my suicide attempt was a cry for help, but I can assure you that it was not. It seemed very real to me. Crying for help is not what I do. I recognise now that my regime may not have achieved my desired outcome, but I believed that it would work, and I was ready to die.

The Psychiatric Unit is a funny old place. I was put into the Bradgate Unit and got a wee room to myself. It had a toilet, which was very necessary, as I was wheeling myself around in a wheelchair at this point and the toilets in the larger units were not easy for me to access.

For my first two weeks in the unit my wife wasn't speaking to me. Sophie didn't want to come and see me, although after a while she did visit. She thought initially it was a ploy for me to get her attention. It wasn't a ploy. I was done – physically and mentally exhausted. Sophie didn't visit often, and when she did she didn't say much. Her friend, Donna, come to visit me quite a lot, which was good of her and she often brought me some nice food. I stayed in my room for the first fortnight I was there. Yeah, I kind of languished there. I didn't receive any specific treatment when I was in the Unit but I took part in pottery classes and I enjoyed speaking to the Occupational Therapist. It felt to me that I had more opportunity to speak to the OT than I did to the nursing staff or doctors on the ward. I had an occupational therapist called Mandy, who was a very nice woman. She did her job perfectly and looked after me well. She got me started onto pottery, and I've got into that and am really enjoying it. I slowly came out of myself and kind of got back to where I was, a little bit chirpier. I still know that I'm not going to get any better from this COPD and to be fair, I still can't be arsed doing very much, but I'm doing my best. I have been going to pottery, Computers for Dummies and guitar lessons.

Being in the Psychiatric Unit for four months, I began to see things a bit more clearly. Sophie and I began to get on a little bit better and around Christmas time I was allowed home for weekends.

It was February and I'd been there nearly four months. I'd still not been discharged but I'd been on home leave for two weekends. I was waiting for things to be finalised for me in the community, like having a Community Psychiatric Nurse set up, classes, a carer or buddy for company, before I got discharged.

People like me, with depression, are ok when they come out of their shell, and you can speak to them. They are on the same level as you to a point, but many of them have added problems related to drugs and alcohol, and some patients are bi-polar or schizophrenic. It can be a bit strange because the drug addicts and alcoholics are quite loud – they kind of take over the place and push the people with depression into the background, as it were. It wasn't until the last three or four weeks that I found my voice and stood up for myself and the others regarding being able to watch TV in peace. It became like Groundhog Day in there. One day led into the other, which led into the next, and nothing seemed to change. The medical staff did change my antidepressants, but they didn't seem to make much of a difference except to make me constipated, which I wasn't before! For the four months I was in the unit I had a sinus infection, which turned into a chest infection, and I'd coughed up and given samples. I'm still on antibiotics. That was nine courses of antibiotics since the beginning of November and still no end in sight. I have now been put on a course of IVs, so hopefully that will clear the infection.

I met a guy, Neil, in the unit who was bipolar and one of the characteristics of his condition was paranoia. I was in the dining room one day and this chap, Neil, came in and sat beside me. I liked him. He was a nice bloke. One of the nurses came along and said the "numpties" were watching *Big Brother* on TV. Neil said to the nurse, "Yeah, "Big Brother" are probably watchin' us."

I said to Neil, "Probably. They've got secret devices and cameras in every bedroom. I've found mine with my electronic sweep and threw it out. "

Of course, I was joking, but Neil started to panic and asked if he could borrow my electronic sweep but I said I'd taken it home. Poor guy, he went into his bedroom and started looking for these bugs. He never found any! One day, Neil warned me not to drink the water because he thought that it was one of the mediums that the staff used to control your mind.

There were some strange looking characters. They looked a bit like zombies from *Sean of the Dead*, or *Dawn of the Dead*. There was an old boy called John who moped around and he was nicknamed 'John of the Dead'.

However, he perked up no end and got out of the Unit before me, in the end. Nice chap. He was doing better than me, all along!

So I was still in the unit but hoping to get home soon.

My tablets seemed to have increased since I went into the unit. I'd have to sort that lot out when I finally got discharged and see what I was happy to take or not. I got pills three times a day: more tablets and compounds than are listed in the Periodic Table. It was phenomenal what I got through. It was ten o'clock, three o'clock and nine o'clock. If I took my dinnertime tablets, that was the bulk of them and the rest were mainly paracetamol.

The food in the unit was rubbish, as per usual. But everything was tidy, I'll say that for the place. The nursing staff were very nice too. Boredom is the main thing for most people in the unit, especially if they can't get out. At least I could leave my room. It was helpful if I could get someone to push my chair as I couldn't walk any more than a couple of minutes before I got pretty out of breath. I started my physiotherapy as well there, although I was finding it really hard. One Tuesday, I walked for two and a half minutes. I had a little 'lean-to' thing which comprised of four wheels to carry my oxygen and a seat for you to sit down on when you are buggered. So, my exercise was to push this lean-to along the corridor with the physiotherapist beside me and I pushed myself to the max – two and a half minutes. What a lot of shite, eh? I had to stop then, and I started to do the dry heave. It just kept coming. I'm in distress in the hospital corridor, and there's all these people looking at me, and the physio is panicking, thinking she's pushed me too far and I'm about to expire on her. And all the while, the heaving continues and I'm trying to be sick. It was horrible. I lost the next two days, because I just felt so bloody ill. I also missed the Friday, as I had to go to the Leicester Royal Infirmary to pick up antibiotics. However, I decided to go back to physio the next Tuesday and in the meantime I would try to do a few weights.

From arriving at the Unit in October to being discharged at the end of February, I had been carrying a nasal infection which was very debilitating and my mood was as miserable as sin. When I got home in February, it was clear that I was no happier than I had been in the October. Sophie couldn't take any more of my miserable mood and needed some space between her and me so she packed her bags and went to stay in a colleague's empty house. I was on several different types of medication for this nasal condition including antibiotics via IV and eventually it cleared up. It would have been better if I'd been given antibiotics intravenously earlier. I don't know why I wasn't.

I'd been watching a tribute to PC David Rathband on TV. He was shot and blinded by Raoul Moat in Northumberland a couple of years before. The chap, Raoul, was finally shot dead by a police marksman. The PC was left blinded and had two glass eyes fitted. I heard that day that he has been found dead in his house. My first thought was that he had committed suicide. It turned out that it was right. The tribute programme on the news was dedicated to him. The interview had been held by a woman called Victoria Derbyshire who worked for Radio 5. She was very good, and she deals with this type of topic. That's her angle. When David Rathband was being interviewed, he said that after his injuries, he wasn't amazed by the help that he got, but by the help he didn't get. Reading between the lines, I kind of guessed that the lack of help was from his family and friends, because he said the nursing staff and the police service had been good, as had his colleagues. However, he said that the people he thought would have helped him didn't. I can relate to that a little bit.

Anyway, he continued to say that he was going to try to keep upbeat and was learning to use a voice recognition computer, and with the help of his wife and family, they would change their ideas and plans to suit their new situation. I thought, "Where have I heard all this before?" Poor chap. He did a couple of different interviews and he'd been on various chat shows to say how positive he was being. However, during these interviews, I thought that his demeanour and body language told a different story. It was really quite sad. I had a funny feeling that he would go downhill. I think his wife left him and took the kids with her. I don't know why that happened. Allegedly he was prone to abusive outbursts, which I can totally understand. The frustration that David Rathband must have felt would be no different to the frustration I feel. When I heard the news of his death that day, I felt heart sorry for him. The guy might not have got the help that he needed. He was probably someone else who'd slipped through the net. Nothing else I could say about him, other than "I hope you've gone off to a better place, mate."

It was my sixth day on IV Tazasin. I was still short of breath and using oxygen but even with the oxygen I had to stop halfway up the stairs in our house. My limbs felt like jelly. I didn't know what was wrong with me. I had no appetite and I had diarrhoea. Probably both down to the antibiotics I was taking. I just felt dreadful. Every time I moved, my legs and arms felt like dead weights and my joints were very painful.

Sophie was tired when she came in from work, so she went to bed to have a bit of a sleep. I was feeling peckish so I went to the kitchen to organise beans on toast for tea. I got as far as the kitchen cupboard and was totally out of breath. I thought, "It's going to take me forever to make beans on toast!" so I had a bag of crisps and a cup of tea and when Sophie got up, she made the beans on toast for me.

Sophie was off to the pub quiz with Donna, which was fine. I just wished she would speak to me a bit more.

I got discharged from the Psychiatric Unit on the Tuesday morning and prior to coming home I met and spoke with my psychiatric nurse who's in the outside world, as it were, for the first time. She seemed nice enough. I'd been out of the Unit for two days and I didn't know whether it was the effects of the IVs or if I was coming down with a virus rather than a bug but I'd slept a lot and cancelled my classes as I couldn't get out of my bed except to make a cup of tea for John the builder and myself and watch the news for an hour. I didn't feel like doing anything, so I thought I'd be as well upstairs in bed. At least if I was upstairs sleeping, my mind would be resting and I was not thinking of where I was presently (and probably always would be). I get a bit of respite in my dreams. I sleep to dream, because in my dreams I'm normal, or better than normal. I'm not in a wheelchair, I'm not gasping for breath – I'm normal Norman again! It could be seen as a waste of a day, but it's a relief. Two days out of the Unit and I was wondering if I could handle being out. Watching that David Rathband tribute had brought the futility of my life back home to me again.

I'd got a couple of days IVs to take. The next Monday and Tuesday I had to go to Rotherham for my photophoresis and if I was not feeling any better I'd go to the Bone Marrow Unit to seek their advice, because I felt as weak as a kitten, to be honest. I didn't know where people got the idea that I was able to do more than I was doing. That view upsets me, because if I could do more, I would do more. When Sophie comes in and asks what I want for tea, I try to keep it simple for her so that she isn't being put upon by me. I don't eat much during the day. I think I've lost the plot again. I'm struggling to see what it's all about.

Ian sent me homework to do, but I was struggling to speak into this Dictaphone on my own. Sophie doesn't really want to talk any more. I seem to do better when I've people around me, like Joyce and Ian. Everything comes out very flat if I'm talking to no-one. I look forward to when we can whiz through the work on the book.

Chapter 17

Dear Diary

3rd March 2012

I've wakened feeling terrible again today. I felt like this yesterday – sickness, headaches, generally feeling rotten, and can't get my breath. Yesterday I took a sleeping tablet and slept through the whole day.

I feel I am on the edge of a panic attack. I tried to tell my wife, but she's as sympathetic as ever. Christ, I'm glad she's not a nurse!

I think I'll probably end up taking another tablet.

Once again, I feel that I'm on my own, in that nobody really gives a fuck about me. As long as all the vital signs are ok, then it seems that I'm ok. But I am on the edge of a panic attack. I've started to get really anxious again. I think it might be time to take another sedative.

I'm just trying to keep everything updated this time. If anyone is in any doubt about how I feel, they're going to get the message, either in this lifetime or the next.

17ᵗʰ March 2012

The shingles continue to be quite disabling. I didn't sleep at all last night, so at ten this morning I took some morphine so I've just woken up from five hours of morphine-induced sleep – and it's now four in the afternoon. Thanks goodness for Oromorph. I really appreciated getting some sleep. But the problem with taking Oromorph is that it makes me constipated – so there will be a payback for using it.

The shingles have moved onto my perineum – the bit between the testes and bottom. It is very painful. The pain around my anus and inside it is quite excruciating, especially when I have to go and empty my bowels.

I've started to get a horribly smelly discharge from my anus and I have messed the bed. Hopefully that will clear up when the shingles go, or I'll have to start wearing a nappy.

Sophie is on nights this week, so she needs to sleep throughout the day. Not that there is anything she can do to change my current situation.

Trevor said he would come over and visit me tomorrow. Good old Trev. That'll cheer me up.

It may seem to some that I always get chest and sinus infections, but as a bonus, I occasionally get shingles too. I've got shingles at the moment, which came about two weeks after my last chest infection. I was free from infection for about ten days, for two of which I felt really quite well. I've now gone a few steps backwards. I've got terrible shingles. I have a blistered area, about the size of a large mug, which runs from my coccyx across the top of my left buttock. It is very sore indeed. Not only that, but the blisters have continued south, down the crack of my arse and have infiltrated my bottom which is absolutely hellish, particularly when I try to go to the toilet. It just hurts so much! I know it sounds like a joke, but I can tell you it's not. If you could have heard me screaming, then whimpering after being to the loo yesterday, I think you might have felt sorry for me. On top of that, there is another pain that goes from the top of my buttock right down my leg to my foot, which is uncomfortable and there all the time, nagging away. So I'm kind of disabled with that at the minute. I have tablets from the Doctor. They didn't want me in the Bone Marrow Unit spreading the shingles virus all over the place. I don't know how long shingles last – it's a chickenpox virus – but the quicker it goes, the bloody better – I can tell you!

John, the builder who has been doing work downstairs on the house for Sophie and I, has finished splitting one room into two. So, we now have a study area and a utility room which will be really nice when it's all painted. Good old Trev has done the electrics and Keith, Sophie's brother, did the plumbing. That helped to keep the cost down a little bit. Once Andy the painter has been in, we'll be good to go.

I don't suppose holidays will come this year, but hopefully Sophie will get the job she is going for in Coventry. If she's successful, it means we can stay in the house we are in at the moment.

I had classes to go to, set up by the Psychiatric Unit, but because of my chest infection and then the shingles, I've not been able to attend.

In between getting the chest infection and the shingles, I went to the Bone Marrow Unit to see Dr Hunter, my old pal. I wasn't getting breath easily despite being on high Vs, and I didn't feel that I was infected. She told me that it could be one of two things – possibly that my body is very tired and run down after trying to get rid of infections for almost four months, just needing time to recover, and hopefully in two or three months' time my breathing will be back to normal for me. Dr Hunter said if it's not back to normal, then it is probably a worsening of my COPD condition – a natural progression of the disease. Not good news. Just something else to cope with.

I've been on the internet, looking for a little electric buggy to help me be more independently mobile. This will save Sophie and Ian, of course, from having to wheel me about. I'd hoped that Sophie and I would be able to go out together but I don't think that will happen, because I feel she doesn't want to be seen with me as an invalid.

Chickenpox is healing up nicely. However, the rash around my backside is not healing up very well. Still very sore going to the loo, but mostly I'm feeling out of breath. I have had a rethink and as far as my symptoms go, Sophie and I think it's very severe thrush. I know that thrush can affect my bronchial passages.

Tues 20th March 2012

Yesterday (Monday) wasn't a good day, pain-wise. I hurt a lot and everything I ate just came right back up. I drank fluids when I could, and in the evening, Rosie came over with a bit of roast beef and trimmings for me and I managed to keep that down. I haven't taken my peg feed the last couple of days, simply because I feel so nauseated. You really don't want to be chucking up peg feed. It's vile.

If I lose a few ounces, so be it.

Rosie has cooked tea again for me tonight and Sophie has just finished her spell on nights. I am trying to make little demands on Sophie. I'm mooching around, drinking tea and watching telly. I don't have the energy for anything else.

I've started on loconosol: thrush treatment medication yesterday, and I'll stick on a high dose of that for a week and see where that takes me.

The cramps in my extremities, excluding my lower legs and feet, are back again today. They are in my right hand and it's being contorted into some strange shapes, but really, what happens to me that doesn't come with pain? Fuckin' sick of it! The cramps in my upper legs in the big muscles are the worst. The pain is so great I could scream, and indeed, I have done. The cramps can last for three or four days, and then not return for a couple of months.

Every few days, I am suffering from something. It's really only me and Sophie who see it. This may not be suitable for the book, but I think there is a place for it. The book is sounding a bit of a laugh, really, but I don't think it's as real as it could be. I'm doing a bit of a diary more regularly, as there is a feeling of despair.

I hope the medicine kicks in and that I'll get a good night's sleep and that tomorrow will be a better day. But I know it fuckin' won't be. Ever the optimist!

Sophie and me

Tues 20th March

I've just had another heartbreaking conversation with my wife again. She is avoiding me, and tonight she's just told me she is going out with her pal tomorrow for the day. Bearing in mind she has just been working a long weekend previously to that, I haven't really been with her since the 9th March. I decided that tonight was the night to find out what was going on in her mind, and if she still wanted to be with me.

She says she doesn't know where she is with this illness and me, and that she can't cope with what it has done to me, and to her. She doesn't know how to cope with us and the situation we are in. I'm in bits. I just want her to put her arms around me, tell me that she loves me, and to spend some time with me. She says that where she is at, at the moment, she just can't do that. She doesn't know if she loves me. More tears on my part. Usually, my eyes can't produce tears. She says she's found it difficult to define the carer and wife role. We've not been intimate, as I've been in hospital for four months and the anti-depressant tablets I'm on are not doing my libido any favours. I don't know if she misses the intimacy. I know that I do.

We also talked about my life expectancy, and that included her wiping my arse and stuff. I hope it never comes to that. I had a feeling myself that I'd be dead by fifty. I really don't want Sophie as a carer. I want her as a wife, but as a wife that loves me. I don't want a wife that stays by my side because she thinks it's the dutiful thing to do. I want Sophie to be there because she wants to be there. I don't want to be ignored by her, but she says she doesn't know what to do when she is around me. I think she is buckling inside. I don't see her as my carer. I've had some intense feelings for Sophie, and she has for me. That includes feeling that we could strangle each other sometimes! I've never loved anybody as deeply as I have loved Sophie, and if what she is going to be is my carer, I don't want to live at all. Our life was never meant to be like this. I think we coped well with the cancer and all that went with it, but we didn't need the GVH in the lungs and the subsequent disabilities that it has brought along with it. That just seems really cruel.

I don't know if our chat is going to do any good ultimately, but this is just another little window into my life. Hopefully things will improve between us. I know that Sophie needs space and time with her pals and I have never minded her doing that. I just wish she would put me on equal footing with her pals, and realise that I love her deeply. I am very content to just be in Sophie's company and would enjoy watching a movie with her at home. Sophie is my rock, and without her to cling to, there is really not any point in me going on. I've fought hard for twenty three years. I'm tired and I feel Sophie is the only thing that keeps me going.

I try to make things better, but I feel I'm always just at the crawling stage as I never seem to get long enough to achieve anything, as the infections just keep coming one after the other and they are getting closer together.

Fri 24th March 2012

Sophie has an appointment to see a heart specialist today. She's had terrible trouble with an irregular heartbeat. She's had the last couple of days off work, which I'm glad of, because she's running herself ragged.

We had a chat the other night and we still don't think that two years is unrealistic for me to live. It depends on what infections I get. If only I could keep myself infection-free! But I can't seem to do that. I'd like to see my fiftieth birthday, but in a reasonable sort of condition.

We seem to have got ourselves sorted again as a couple and are understanding a bit more where each of us is coming from. She needs to talk to me more. Sophie has always found pushing me in the wheelchair difficult and I've never wanted to be in a wheelchair anyway, so the next plan is to get an electric scooter so that nobody has to push me at all. It's lightweight and breaks down into component parts.

I had the GP out today. It was a long visit, and the first I've had since all this began when I was twenty five. The GP was here about the pain I was getting from shingles and suspected thrush, constipation and my increasing lack of breath. I was glad the doctor came to me, as I was feeling crap. The GP gave me 5mls of gel for my constipation and within 10 minutes of inserting the gel, I was in the loo and things were cleared! Now that's what I call efficient!

Sophie is going off to see her pal Penny tonight. She is really nice and is going to have her second baby at forty four years old. I wish she'd befriend Sophie more regularly.

Healthwise, today has not been good. Hopefully I can get some sleep tonight.

I've decided to grow a handlebar moustache!

Chapter 18

Weekend was reasonably comfortable. I managed some sleep with the aid of sleeping tablets. Spent most of Sunday in bed.

Still not getting my breath very easily.

Donna still persists in making her presence felt. She came round today and Donna and Sophie went out with Duncan the dog for a couple of hours. I was upstairs, so she didn't really bother me. Sophie came back after her two hour walk with Donna and spent the afternoon doing her presentation, and it would appear that Donna has been texting her most of the afternoon and evening. So whilst I've been thinking that Sophie is doing her presentation and that I should leave her in peace, she has actually been texting Donna.

There still isn't a great deal of chat between Sophie and me. Its same old, same old. She's here, but she's not communicating much. Sophie's just announced that Donna has asked her to go on holiday with her in April for ten days to Sharm el Sheikh. Five hundred and fifty pounds, all inclusive. Bit of a bargain – I suppose she should go really.

One time when Sophie visited me in Glenfield Psychiatric Unit, we agreed that we should each write a list of 10 things that might help our situation, and one of my suggestions was that Sophie should go on holiday with some friends. I thought she would be fed up in my company and that a few breaks away with friends throughout the year would do her the world of good. But she's had various breaks and still is rarely in my company. I did say to Donna that she saw more of my wife than I did. She hasn't been round to the house since I said that. I thought that was 'Advantage: Norman', but I forgot about technology! They also get to see each other at work, too. What can I do? I'm only the husband. Donna's husband,

Mark, has completely blown her out of the water. He doesn't want to be friends or anything with her.

I have my psychiatric visit at the hospital tomorrow. First one since being discharged.

I've got a new electric buggy so I will try that out tomorrow.

Sophie is off to meet someone at Coventry, prior to her interview on Thursday.

28th March 2012

Sophie had a job interview today in Coventry and she's just told me that she got the job, which is great.

Sophie's home and we've had a chat. Things are no different, in that Sophie says everything is all my fault, because she says I speak to her like shit. The fact that I've hardly spoken to her since she started the preparations for her Leicester Royal interview way back, until today, when she got interviewed for the job in Coventry, seems to have escaped her. Sophie says I'm always complaining about being ill, but it's only if she asks that I tell her how I'm feeling; for example, that I've got a sore stomach. I think I've not been complaining. Other people tell me that I seem a bit better.

I've been out in the garden.

Picked up my guitar again today, after a long break.

Sophie's been advised by the doctors at the Psychiatric unit to get her own counselling. Of course, she's done absolutely nothing about it.

Sophie has told me that she'd rather be in Donna's company than mine, which isn't heartening. She said she'd rather be in anyone else's company but mine. She says she feels trapped, but can't do anything about it. When I asked her why she doesn't divorce me, she says, "Well, how can I divorce you?"

I asked why she would put herself through this, if it's that bad. Sophie has the financial means to look after herself. It's me who will struggle, not Sophie.

I think I'm making great efforts to keep things on an even keel but Sophie thinks I'm as bad as ever. I wonder where she is coming from, sometimes. If she really doesn't want to be with me, I don't want to be under the same roof as her, either. She may want to sort something out regarding accommodation. I'll not initiate anything. I feel angry at Sophie's behaviour, but she won't discuss the situation with me. She says there's no point. Today is the first time since being discharged from the Psychiatric Unit that I have got angry.

I thought that when Sophie got the job in Coventry, the sweat would be off and things might have settled back down, but obviously not. When Sophie got back from her successful interview, I invited her out for dinner, but she seemed to imply that there was no point, as I would just call off at the last minute.

Sophie spends a lot of time with Donna, eye to eye, texting and phoning.

Sophie is in denial about something. It's about me. She won't tell me what she wants to do about me. Her behaviour is impacting on my health again. I think she is the one who's being unfair.

I know I won't be able to let this lie.

Thursday 30ᵗʰ March 2012

My shingles and thrush are all clearing up, so that's good news.

I assumed that with Sophie getting her job that we could go out tonight and celebrate together. I couldn't think about where to go, but came up with the idea of Ashfields, about six o'clock tonight. It's quite a posh restaurant. I mentioned it to Sophie but she said that she wanted to go to the Bricklayers Arms for something to eat. Due to being on the big heavy tank of oxygen, I wanted to go somewhere quiet, with few people. The Bricklayers Arms is usually very busy.

Anyway, it transpired that Sophie wanted to go to the Brickies to meet Donna and a few other friends to celebrate her success. I was welcome to come if I wanted, or to stay at home. I've opted for the stay at home version. I don't know what I've done. Just when I think there is a little bit of hope for us, she comes out with a curve ball like that. I don't know where I stand. For one night, we could have gone somewhere nice. I'd have shaved and put on something reasonably dressy – certainly clean! Anyway, she's gone off out, now. I hope she has a great night. She probably will.

I think we are back to square one again. Less snot and tears on my part. I wish she would just make a clean cut of our relationship as it were.

I'm looking forward to Joyce and Ian coming next week. I don't know if Sophie will want to be involved. Might sell my car. I fancy something else.

March 31st 2012

Saturday 31st March, my wife and I sat down together to speak about where our relationship was going. I told her that I wasn't prepared to live under the same roof as her, as she was treating me terribly. Sophie said it would easier to speak to her friend and ask if she could live in their empty house, which they keep for guests and visitors.

On Sunday 1st April, Sophie went to live in her friend's spare house. April Fool.

Sophie thinks that there has been no improvement in my mood since I came home from the Psychiatric Unit, whereas I think I've been doing ever so well. Clearly, we are not seeing it the same way. So, Sophie has gone. I am glad I broached the subject of our relationship.

Sophie kept insisting that she couldn't go, and asked

who would look after me, but on the Saturday night after we had been discussing everything, Sophie went out with her pals and never came home that night. I was very worried about her. Sophie did send me a text but I didn't get it till the next morning. Seemingly, Sophie had got drunk and couldn't drive home and stayed overnight with her friend, Andrea.

On the Sunday, Sophie packed and left for the spare house.

She insisted on taking me to the hospital on Monday 2nd April to meet with my consultant, Dr Ann Hunter. The appointment date had been brought forward and a special appointment had been set up. This, in itself, was unusual. It was also unusual that Dr. Hunter wanted to see me. She normally left me to more junior doctors these days. When the appointment was changed, I said to Sophie that I thought something was going on. But Sophie said, "No, no! Dr Murray could be on study leave," so I didn't give it much more thought. Although it was also odd that Sophie was coming with me and joined in the meeting. Some time ago, Sophie and I had agreed that it would be unlikely for me to see my 50th birthday.

Dr Hunter asked, "How are you feeling?" When I told her, she said, "I don't think that haematology is the best place for your treatment, as the treatment we've been giving you is no longer working." I frowned, wondering where this left me, but she added, "I feel that the Photophoresis treatment you are getting at Rotherham hospital is no longer working, judging by the amount of infections you are still getting."

So my treatment there would be phased out. I have to admit that I was finding the travelling to Rotherham very tiring. My treatment at Rotherham spanned two days, so I stayed in a hotel in Rotherham overnight. Latterly, however, I was unable to get to the hotel restaurant for my evening meal, as I was so out of breath. Dr Hunter also said that even with the best drugs they were giving me, I was not getting free of infection. My immune system is basically buggered, and she suggested that my care be handed over to LOROS McMillan, and for it to be more palliative in nature. This shift to LOROS McMillan came as quite a shock to me as I have always associated the word palliative with hospice and hospice with death.

I hate that word: 'hospice' – it just sounds so final! I was very anxious about this change in my care and said so to Dr Hunter. Dr Hunter offered to arrange for me to speak to a specialist at LOROS, who would talk through with me all the things that I was anxious about. Dr Hunter assured me that the Palliative Care staff were well up with pain relief and infection control and would be able to identify what care I would need, going forward. It felt a bit as though I was getting pushed out of the door. It's true that I don't feel well and Dr Hunter has rightly identified that I am going downhill. I'm no sooner clear of one infection than another comes along. Sophie told Dr Hunter that we were on a trial separation. Dr Hunter said she was very shocked, as she always saw Sophie and I as a strong team and we pulled for each other. I guess even the strongest teams get beaten, eventually. I explained to Dr Hunter that I was incredibly upset about the whole thing, but that I couldn't blame Sophie.

I have a hospice nurse coming to visit me this Wednesday.

I feel as though the rug has been pulled from under my feet. The meeting was a bit of a shocker. I get the impression that the drugs aren't going to work and I don't have a terribly long time to go. For me, I'm just sad that my marriage just couldn't have gone the course. Even if Sophie came back, and was nice to me, and was like a wife (which I don't think will happen), I think I would be walking around on eggshells. I don't think she will be back.

Sophie brought me back to the house after our joint meeting with Dr Hunter, and I asked her if she had expected the meeting to be as it was. She admitted that she thought Dr Hunter might have difficult things to say. I was a bit put out, because when I suggested that possibility to Sophie prior to the meeting, Sophie denied it. I wish people would be honest and let the truth come out as the person's illness or disease progresses! For me, at least, that would be an easier way to deal with it, rather than people holding back from telling it how it is. Sophie left after doing a couple of chores in the house, and was off.

I am now stuck here on my own. I sometimes go to our neighbours, Rosie and Jeff, but today I thought I wouldn't do that. It feels as though I would be going cap in hand to them because Sophie has left. Rosie and Jeff are already incredibly kind to me and to Sophie. Jeff calls in each day to take my dog for a walk and says "hi" to me, and Rosie often made a meal for me and Sophie to have in the evening.

I feel really alone.

I have my oxygen on a lot of the time. I have yet another infection that the tablets can't get rid of, and neither can my immune system. Yeah, I think I am going downhill.

Dr Hunter says I've to go back to see her at the end of the month – 30th April.

My care is with the Palliative care people, not because I'm dying, but so that they can organise better home help etc. I've been assessed for a care package, which will take a bit of time, so I'm in limbo at the minute. It would be good if I got some help, because due to my breathlessness and arthritis, I can barely lift any weight. The buggy that I've got to help me be mobile is split into 4 separate pieces, but the bit that holds the motor is heavy and by the time I lift that into the car, I am absolutely buggered. So I really need somebody to lift it into the car, and then, on arrival at my destination, I need someone to lift the parts out of the car and build up the buggy so that I can get about and enjoy a whiz round the country park on the level ground. I might try and find out about other railway walks where the paths are tarmac. I might do that when I go to Scotland.

Thursday 5th April

I am feeling very out of breath. I've been to the toilet and back and it's floored me – and that's with oxygen on. It kind of scares me, because the slightest effort makes it very

266

hard to breathe. I feel very distressed about it all.

There hasn't been anything in the way of contact since Sophie left. Not from anybody, except Joyce. Trevor has been a bit of a stalwart. He's been popping round, despite his stump being sore and raw and giving him a bit of a problem. He's had to get his wife Linda to drive him around. Cheers, Trevor.

Chapter 19

1st June 2012

Sophie's done her bit for my book by agreeing to the audio taped interview with me. I can remember the rest.

I suppose I have never really accepted my illness and moved on. Deep down, I've always had the "Why me?" question in my mind. Sophie says I've been grumpy and angry all the way through our marriage and she's taken it on the chin. I've always shouted and ranted and railed against my ill health – and life in general. I remember a Martial Arts instructor telling me of an old Chinese proverb which, he said, described me. It went something like, "In life, certain types of people are like a tree that stood up to the strongest wind. Slowly, the tree would lose its branches, snapping off in the wind until there were no branches left. It was just the trunk that remained. Whereas other people are like blades of grass – they would bend with the wind and therefore didn't get broken by the wind." So, rather than tackle things head on, as I always have done, standing immovably, I should maybe have tried going with the flow and tried to accept or deflect things, rather than stand straight up and rail against them. Bolted horse and all that!

So, it's now the 1st June, 2012, and my marriage has been very unstable for the past eighteen months, mainly due to me not being able to accept my health situation.

When Sophie went away to stay in her colleagues house, I missed her terribly. I phoned her and asked her to come home because I wasn't coping. She duly did. This was at the beginning of April 2012.

Sophie herself had done really well in her professional capacity and had recently been appointed as a Consultant at Coventry Hospital. She was due to take up her new post in July 2012 and was keen to live close to the hospital in Coventry during the week and come back home at weekends. We agreed to release funds from the equity on our marital home to allow this to happen. At this point a care package began to be sorted out between Psychiatric Care and the Social Work Department. This would allow me to have some support during the day in relation to shopping, cooking, laundry and so on, especially when Sophie was at work in Coventry. Whilst I was very disappointed that Sophie was going to live in Coventry during the week, I could understand the sense in her living close to the hospital and the need to get away from me. Things were still not right between us at this point in April.

I had an appointment to go and see the Specialist at LOROS, a Dr Luke Feathers, who explained to me the service that LOROS offered. I had a lot of concerns going from a mainstream Medical Model to a situation where a Palliative Model was the main agenda. I was scared about what this meant for me and asked Dr Feathers outright, "How long have I actually got to live?"

Dr Feathers told me that I might only have a year to live; maybe less if an infection took hold. I can see, looking back, that my disease (COPD) had slowly progressed and I am now unable to do a great deal which I find very frustrating. However, Dr Feathers was the first person to tell me "Look, this disease is going to kill you." It was the first time I took it on board. At the special meeting with Dr Hunter, she did say that maybe it was time for me to stop fighting my condition and just to take things more easily. I don't know a better way to describe what she said but it sounded to me that the medics felt they had done their best and that the inevitable is round the corner. Maybe it is, but the problem is that I just don't seem able to give up fighting to live! Sophie was with me at this appointment and obviously got the news as well. I remember trying to be brave and doing quite well till I got home and then I just burst into tears. Sophie and I were sitting on the bed and she gave me a hug, saying things would be ok, and we'd see it through together. Our marriage had been miserable for the last eighteen months and although this news was awful, it gave me hope that we could put the misery behind us and do the last leg of the journey together.

The state of my health has always been a worry to me but the state of our marriage was causing me a whole lot more pain. A different kind of pain. So I was glad that it seemed to me that we'd put the bad stuff behind us and we were saying that we would work together again. Sophie had explained to me why she had left me to go and stay in her colleague's house and had expressed why she'd had enough. I found her explanation helpful and thought we had managed to put the bad stuff behind us. So although the prognosis was not good, I was so glad that our marriage seemed to be in a better place.

Since a loose measure has been put on the time I have left, it has clarified for me just how bad I have become, health-wise. I realise that with a limited amount of time, I should be relaxing a bit and taking things easy. I have done all I can. There is nothing else left for me to do, other than to try and get my house in order, and that is what I have started to do. I am hoping to get things sorted so that there isn't a lot for Sophie to do after my demise. I know there is nothing worse than emptying the contents of a loved one's cupboards, drawers, garage, or whatever. I know that I am nostalgic about stuff and don't know what to throw away, but I'm hoping to make all those decisions for Sophie and use what time we have to be together, work together and be happy together.

At this point I'd made up my mind to stop railing, being angry and stop fighting my condition, so instead of being like the tree, I'd try to be like the blade of grass. I wanted to try and make everything right with Sophie and make the remaining time together as nice as possible. I thought that was what we were working on, because Sophie was telling me that we would sort things out together, everything would be OK, and our situation wouldn't be a worry. But although she was saying these words, I noticed that her body language was telling me something else – if I went to give her a hug or a cuddle, or patted her bottom, she would cringe and roll away from me. I don't know if she felt that she was being touched by a complete stranger or what, but she didn't want me around or near her. She would make any excuse to go off with her pals rather than be with me and this was breaking my heart. I knew there was something going on in her head, but she's telling me different. The week of the 29th June, 2012 had been difficult as she wouldn't talk to me when she was at home and frequently went out to be with other people. There was no ranting and raving on my part. I was just sorry that Sophie was being really cold towards me.

Eventually, I asked her if she would sit down and tell me what was going on and she said at that point, that our marriage was basically done, and that she doesn't want to be in my company. I am devastated, as I really thought we could get back on track and that we could see the journey through to the end together, as we'd recently discussed following my special appointment. But now Sophie is going to live in Coventry during the week, in a house bought with some of the equity of our joint home, and I learn that Sophie has forgotten to put my name on the deeds of her new house. Sophie says she will come back at the weekends, but if she does, and chooses not to talk or to be near me, then it's as though she isn't really here at all. I think over time she will stop coming back. I feel very sad, vulnerable and very frightened.

I have just recently finished going through all the medical stuff that has happened to me following my bone marrow transplant. I thought I'd hit rock bottom when my lungs collapsed and are now so damaged. I didn't think anything else could hurt me more. I was wrong. My marriage has gone now.

I know I am going to have to get on without her, but

I don't want to get on without her! I really have no other reason to want to go on. I feel hopeless: so low, so alone. I feel like I did when she first left me. I feel sick, and my stomach is in knots. I feel I have tried everything to remain married to Sophie, short of begging and crawling on my knees. I don't know what else to do to make her see how sorry I am that she has had to go through all this, and that when I was ranting and raving, although it was her who was getting it in the ear, it wasn't her who was the problem: it was my ill health.

Sophie says it's been too much and she just can't do it anymore. Last night, I was sobbing in bed and got up for some tissues. Sophie was in her room, awake in bed. I asked her why she didn't come through to see me when I was upset and she said that she doesn't know what to say to me, and because of that, she felt that doing nothing seemed a more appropriate response. I knew then that I was banging my head against a wall – our marriage was never going to get back to where it had been. Maybe if I was honest with myself, I might have seen this situation coming sooner, but I didn't. Bolted horses – stable doors. I have apologised to Sophie on so many occasions, but she says all she can manage is that we can still be friends, and that she'll come back at weekends to see how I am. I'm devastated. I feel completely devoid and empty.

I continue to go to LOROS for counselling every couple of weeks and this has been very helpful. I'm adjusting – again – to another change in my life and hope I can manage this new situation, as I've done so many times before.

Chapter 20

I am going to start around July 2012. So I will take it from there.

In July, Sophie stopped putting any of her salary into the joint account. She never told me: I found out months and months afterwards, around October or November, and again, it was only down to my prudence that we never went overdrawn. She did put in the mortgage money for that period, but no extras went in, even after my wife telling me that I wouldn't be out of pocket. If it wasn't for me being frugal with the pennies, then I might have been.

My wife had always said she would come back at the weekends and make sure everything was OK, and that was agreed. But round about the same time, in July or August she made it clear that she wouldn't be coming back as a wife, but just to see if I was alright. I found this very unhelpful and was upset, but worse, her coming back at weekends didn't continue for more than a month. Then she said that she didn't want to do that, either. She did come home to do her washing and go on the computer, but would go out with her pals and stay out all night, and never let me know. She would rather go out with Quentin, her old boss, than be in my company.

There was no housework for her to do, since all of that was taken care of during the week by my PAs, so it's not as if she had the drudgery of housework to do. Her time was free time, really, but she didn't want to spend it with me.

The worst thing was her going out and not coming back. I didn't know where she was, and I would wait up until the small hours for her to come home. She didn't. I couldn't understand why she went out with Quentin! He was one of her bosses at the LRI, and according to Sophie, he had stabbed her in the back. She was very quick to forgive him!

I must admit, all this emotional upheaval – one minute, her coming home, and the next minute going out with other people and staying out all night – was taking its toll on me physically and mentally. And then, I think it was the end of August, she said she could no longer come home regularly; she wanted her freedom and didn't want to be tied down with a disabled man.

She wants to enjoy herself and can't do that with me.

So you can imagine how I felt then, at the end of August. I was devastated, really. She even took the dog, Duncan, in September. I asked her not to, but she took him anyway. I did take a rare trip out, to go to the house in Coventry to ask for Duncan back, because she was at work and the dog would be left all day and would suffer. She said she had arranged a dog walker for £60 per week, and with that, I was told to leave without him. She did that for about a month. Then Duncan was returned to me at the end of September. She said she could no longer look after him and that £240 a month for a dog walker was overly expensive. I had tried to tell her that! So that got me the two dogs again – Max, the German Shepherd dog, and Duncan. The dogs are happy enough, with Geoff looking after Max and walking him.

At the end of September, beginning of October, Sophie's Mum tried to persuade Sophie to treat me a bit better. She returned at the weekends, being really, really nice to me, very warm, and I foolishly thought things were getting a bit better and that her Mum had succeeded in persuading her that things were not all that bad. I never thought they were, to be fair. Her Mum came to stay for the week, and Sophie was super-nice to me, and even her Mum could see the difference in her daughter.

Lesley professed that it was a good sign, trying to assure me that I was loved by her like a son, and saying that I was one of the family. She told mutual friends this, too. So that was nice, and I felt that I was getting warmth and support there.

Sophie's Mum left and immediately, Sophie started to treat me like shit again. I was getting really fed up with all the ups and downs, and my health suffered. It was giving me anxiety and panic attacks that affected me physically and I was feeling really, really unwell: retching and I had nausea all the time, just feeling absolutely dreadful. I really don't know how else to put it. I felt so bad that I was admitted into LOROS – the hospice – for a little respite care and TLC. I really was on an emotional roller coaster – one minute up; one minute down. It got the better of me.

Sophie came up to the Hospital and called into the Hospice to see me.

"Why the change?" I asked Sophie. "First you're OK with me again, and then, when your Mum goes you change!"

She looked down at her hands, finding them suddenly fascinating, "I was just putting on a show to keep Mum off my back. You just read too much into it."

I fumed, unable to speak to her.

"Norman, you'd really be better off in a home, you know," Sophie suggested. "You should consider it."

You know, something inside me died, right then. I knew that that this was a real turning point. She had left me and broken my heart, but her suggestion that I go into a home! It was as if she wasn't satisfied with that. She was now going to try and break my spirit.

"Just get out. Please."

I asked Sophie to leave at that point because all that her presence brought me was cold comfort. That was the game changer for me. She wasn't breaking my spirit!

Her Mum, Lesley, came back after the talks and visiting me at LOROS and offered to give my dog Max a permanent home with her. I was delighted with this, because Max doted on Lesley, and she liked Max, and I knew that he would be going to a good home.

I have not heard anything from Lesley since. She took my dog and I don't know how he is. I have not heard a thing, to this day, from the Julian family – including her brothers, her stepfather, John, or her Mum, which I find strange, because you know, she was supposed to love me like a son. And Daniel and Keith were supposed to love me like brothers.

Well so much for that. I am disappointed, bitterly disappointed in that. November came, and with it, Joyce, down to give me a bit of moral support.

Under the circumstances, I thought to myself, "I'd better take £5,000 out of the joint savings."

That was just under half of what was in there, and with that, I had to cover any costs of a stair lift I was getting fitted, Christmas in general, and the other bits and bobs that mount up around Christmas time. Now, initially, Sophie didn't seem too bothered, saying she hoped I would spend the money on something nice. But then she went really funny. She came round here accusing me of stealing her money. Trevor was here, fortunately

"That wasn't your money to take!" she yelled. "That was money I put in this month!"

I informed her that I had put money into the bank from the sale of a Segway, a motor generator and various other bits and bobs from the garage. I had actually put in an extra £4,400 added to a sum of £3,600. I was quite within my rights to take out £5,000, but no – she never ever saw it like that. She reckoned I should have had half of £5000 and the rest was hers.

So Sophie then did something really nasty. Bearing in mind she had not put money into the joint account since July, she went into the joint account and cleared it of £1000 – all that was in it, which was my benefits money for the month – and then she didn't pay the mortgage for two months! Unfortunately, I didn't realise that the Co-op joint account was now overdrawn, and I got charges amounting to over £300. I had to very quickly set up new debits, which was a big inconvenience.

I remember that I tried for six weeks to speak to Sophie about all this, but she just blanked me completely. In the end, I had to go and see a solicitor who told me the only way that I was going to get things organised was to get a divorce underway. Sometime in May 2012, Sophie had managed to get me to sign half the equity of the house over to her so she could buy a property in Coventry. She took out £117,500. That's about £20,000 more than she is entitled to, because as it stands at the moment, we would get about £95,000 each from our marital home, which is jointly owned.

I knew she was buying a house in Coventry, but was under the impression that my name would be on the deeds. Yet I had a look at the paperwork one day when Sophie was at work, and discovered that my name wasn't on the deeds. The only recourse I had was to either get her to sign half of it over to me, which she wasn't going to do, or divorce her.

So that's what happened initially, that persuaded me to get the solicitor involved. My wife refused to accept this and re-petitioned for her own divorce. I remember that Christmas was a pretty grim one. I was upset with all that had gone on and I had received no Christmas cards from Sophie or any of her family. But my friends Geoff and Rosemary invited me over for Christmas dinner, which was good of them. I think I got the invite on the 23rd for the 25th, with them leaving the invitation open in case I got invited by someone else.

Yes January 14th sticks in my mind. Sophie rejected my divorce petition and submitted her own. I remember being upset at that, again. The Solicitor advised me just to accept it for the sake of speed, given that I was told by the doctors that I have about a year to live. She said that it can make a difference to the financial settlement, so I was told to get the house valued and collate all my financial documents, ISA savings certificates and everything, so the solicitor could sort out a financial settlement. My wife was supposed to do the same, but she didn't.

The only good thing about it was that she started to repay half the mortgage in February, so that was a huge help. She could have paid more, but I wasn't going to get more than half out of her. As I say, it's not enough, but it's something. I can just keep my head above water.

Just about then, Joyce and Noreen visited me, and later, Joyce and her daughter, my niece Sally, came for a visit, which was a nice break from the norm. Joyce and I had been working on the book and we both decided we had done as much as we could to try to move this book on, and the only way it was ever to get finished was to find an editor, so that's what happened. We couldn't do it any justice so I went on the web and found two or three editors. A couple got back to me. One read a shortened version of it and got back to me to say he didn't want the job, and then I spoke to Linda, and to be honest, she was very upbeat, so we plumped for her. We read the terms, and the book was underway. That was fine and both Joyce and I were relieved that that had been taken out of our hands.

In February, I was still seeing my counsellor, Rosemary, every fortnight. I found this really helpful, although we were coming to the end of it by then. She was making me see things in a different light and helping me to see a way forward. Rosemary was retiring, and when she did, we would wind up the sessions and by then I should be A-OK.

As it turned out, I was reasonably well. Rosemary has been retired for two months and my head is mostly above water. I try not to let things drag me down and I am feeling better now, both physically and mentally. People have noticed the difference, so that is good; I must be doing something right.

Anyway, back to the February of 2013. I think I had gone out for a rare pint one Friday night, having been picked up by my friends Donna and Robert at about 8pm, aiming to be back for 10pm. When I got home, I couldn't put my finger on it, but something wasn't right about the house. I went to my bed wondering what it was, and when I got up in the morning, I was going downstairs when I suddenly thought, "Pictures are missing!"

My wife had been in, during the two hours I'd been away and actually removed stuff from the house! I found myself getting quite angry at that. She'd told me I wasn't welcome at the house in Coventry and I wasn't to turn up unannounced. I asked her to give me the same thing in return: not to turn up to my house unannounced. She didn't stick to her bargain and helped herself to prints and things off the walls.

About three weeks later, I went out again and when I came back in, there were more things missing. So this was now the end of February and she was still not talking to me or the Solicitor. Come March, I started going to LOROS as a day club. It's a bit dull but the staff are nice and I can go up there and read the paper and have a sandwich and a drink. I can have a chat with them, and it's an afternoon out, so that's OK. Joyce says she will lend me the money if I have to pay the Solicitors, since it's looking like I am going to need some financial support, because legal aid won't cover it. The Solicitor says it could cost anything between £3,000 and £12,000 plus VAT, which I haven't got, so Joyce has offered to bail me out. I will owe her that, and I think when I pass on the house will be sold, and Joyce will get her money back that way. That's what I have agreed to do, anyway, so that way I'm not scratching around and robbing Peter to pay Paul, sort of thing.

Again, in March, I rang up the council about employing my own Personal Assistants (Carers). I have been along to see them and it seems quite straightforward. MIND, the company that currently supplies the people, are a useless bloody lot. If your carer goes sick they can't find replacements and you're left on your own. Once in a blue moon that's OK, but it seems to happen frequently, so looking after my own interests seems the way to go. I shall be looking into that further.

In April, Joyce comes for another visit which is something to look forward to and Linda is moving forward with the book. We are all pleased about the book which is taking shape quicker than I had anticipated, to be honest. That's good. The only thing about April is the PEG feed I get overnight (basically, a bag of food into my stomach). By morning when it's finished, I wake up feeling bloated, sick and nauseated. We have tried to change the food and the rate, and at this time I am only on half the food I should be and not taking enough in orally. This means I am losing a bit of weight, but my weight has been up and down for a long time now. We are on a downward turn at present, but you know, good time and bad times.

Well that's me now and the first draft of the book has been sent off to be critiqued by various people.

Unfortunately I have had to pay to take Sophie to court and have had to hire myself a barrister. Hopefully I can see it through in as short a time as possible. Again, Joyce has agreed to fund me, so it's a real shame, because it should never have got to this point. My wife could have had everything. I still had the original will, leaving everything to her. It was stupid of her. All I wanted was for her to come home at weekends and treat me in a civil fashion. She had made it clear that she no longer considered sleeping with me an option, which was another blow, but to be honest, at the time that suited me anyway with my condition – out of breath and all. So she could have had it all, but now she is going to lose it all. After speaking to the Solicitor in December 2012 I changed my will leaving my wife nothing.

Sometime in April 2013 Trevor turned up at the house with his suitcase, saying, "I'm not getting any respect at home, and I'm not going back until I do!"

He stayed for about four weeks and he was very helpful. He cut the grass, and sat with me and watched the TV and that was fine, and after four weeks he had sorted it out with his family and stepsons and they all agreed to try again and make a go of it this time. That's good and

I'm pleased for them all.

I am my own boss from July 1st because I will employ my own personal assistants. I have one of my old PAs, Rhonda and a new girl Christina, and Trevor has agreed to help me out at weekends. I'm looking forward to that. It will be good, and hopefully will mean going onwards and upwards.

My divorce is still progressing slowly but I am confident that I will get a just decision and equal share – so I just keep on keeping on!

Into the unknown.

The only person you ever really know is yourself – and even then, you can still surprise yourself. And if there are still ladies out there who are struggling to get their boobs moisturised, I may be able to help you out; but be warned, I'm quite slow these days.

Epilogue

The purpose of this book through Norman's eyes was to share his fight against severe illness over a long period of time while still trying to get on with his life. In spite of the trauma of illness he reduced the fear, suffering and anger with infectious humour. Perseverance was the name of his game. Sadly, Norman died on 27th September, 2013. He will be greatly missed.

Lightning Source UK Ltd.
Milton Keynes UK
UKOW05f0704030214

225751UK00012B/169/P